FROM
ELDER
TO
ANCESTOR

"Western culture is death-phobic and age-phobic. We have jettisoned the ancient concept of eldering, leaving older individuals to feel "past it." Unfortunately, little effort is made for our communities to tap into the Well of Wisdom (*Mímisbrunnr* in Norse cosmology) that elders draw upon. I only wish this important book had been available decades ago! It offers a roadmap for restoring ancient pathways in the human psyche. Bless the collective by living well and dying well, becoming a well elder and well Ancestor."

IMELDA ALMQVIST, TEACHER OF SACRED ART & SEIÐR,
AND AUTHOR OF *SACRED ART* AND *NORTH SEA WATER IN MY VEINS*

"I have followed S. Kelley Harrell's work since her early beginnings as a shaman, healer, and author. In *From Elder to Ancestor*, Harrell's innovative style of pedagogy, goodwill toward diverse communities, and visionary directives are clear, prescient, and ready to inspire and motivate all who partake. If you seek a greater understanding of matters of the spirit and your role, you must read this book."

PRIESTESS STEPHANIE ROSE BIRD, BLACK NATURALIST,
SPIRITUAL HEALER, AND AUTHOR OF *MOTHERLAND HERBAL*

"*From Elder to Ancestor* offers essential guidance for those of us living in the fallout of settler colonialism, the abandonment of ritual, and the violent disruption of our relationship to our bodies, the land, and our more-than-human allies. Harrell compassionately guides us in exploring the wounds this forced separation has left in us and with great care and wisdom illuminates pathways through those wounds back into deep, joyful relationship and true community. She provides a clear blueprint for becoming an elder and Ancestor our descendants would be proud of through inspiring reflection questions and practical exercises and teaches us to become someone capable of being a bridge to a future worthy of the next generations who are coming. This book is a much needed antidote to the poison of divisiveness and disconnection that characterizes so much of the times we are in."

LANGSTON KAHN, SHAMANIC PRACTITIONER
AND AUTHOR OF *DEEP LIBERATION*

"*From Elder to Ancestor* is a breakthrough and the first book I have encountered that skillfully describes animism—our interdependence with nature and the spirit world—as inseparable from our journey to becoming true elders and Ancestors. Harrell takes an in-depth look at colonialism as 'the broken path' and, with integrity and compassion, offers wisdom on healing trauma, claiming the Sacred Self, 'eldering well,' cosmology, lore, reciprocity with nature, and ancient practices on the land. Thank you, S. Kelley Harrell, for a brilliant book that captures the essence of our vital reconnection to Earth, soul, and the perennial cycles of life."

PEGI EYERS, AUTHOR OF *ANCIENT SPIRIT RISING*

"*From Elder to Ancestor* offers the path to be remembered back into a "real person"—one who is aware of being irrevocably woven into the fabric of all that is. In being consciously connected again and aware of your internal speed bumps, you will be able to find your own way to implement positive, creative action in the world in harmony with all the rest of our Naturekin."

EVELYN C. RYSDYK, TEACHER OF SHAMANIC SPIRITUALITY AND AUTHOR OF *THE NORSE SHAMAN*, *SHAMANIC CREATIVITY*, AND *SPIRIT WALKING*

"This book is a fascinating deep dive into a worldview that embraces wholeness and the sacredness of the world, encouraging each of us to find our place within both our present and future community. It frames elderhood not as a title but as an action—a role that we can fill through compassion and right action."

MORGAN DAIMLER, AUTHOR OF *FAIRYCRAFT AND TRAVELLING THE FAIRY PATH*

"A must-read for anyone who cares about themselves, others, the world, the present, and the future. This book draws you into the very real and often neglected conversation about how we are, and have always been, Nature and bound to each other as such. Separation is an illusion and a tool of oppressors, and by encouraging a deep and thoughtful journey, Harrell helps us begin to break free from limited thinking. This conversation is important and vital. From the Rite of Heartbreak to revaluing reciprocity and community, Harrell has us step back into where we should have always been: a part of creating a future and being a good Ancestor."

IRISANYA MOON, AUTHOR OF *GAIA* AND *THE NORNS*

FROM
ELDER
TO
ANCESTOR

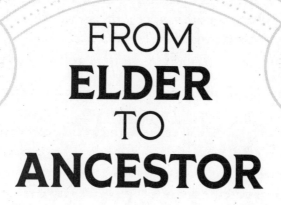

Nature Kinship for All Seasons of Life

S. Kelley Harrell

Destiny Books
Rochester, Vermont

Destiny Books
One Park Street
Rochester, Vermont 05767
www.DestinyBooks.com

Destiny Books is a division of Inner Traditions International

Cataloging-in-Publication Data for this title is available from the Library of Congress

ISBN 978-1-64411-662-3 (print)
ISBN 978-1-64411-663-0 (ebook)

Printed and bound in the United States by Lake Book Manufacturing, LLC

10 9 8 7 6 5 4 3 2 1

Text design and layout by Debbie Glogover
This book was typeset in Garamond Premier Pro with Gill Sans MT Pro and
Tiller used as display typefaces

To send correspondence to the author of this book, mail a first-class letter to the
author c/o Inner Traditions • Bear & Company, One Park Street, Rochester, VT
05767, and we will forward the communication, or contact the author directly at
soulintentarts.com.

Scan the QR code and save 25% at InnerTraditions.com.
Browse over 2,000 titles on spirituality, the occult, ancient
mysteries, new science, holistic health, and natural medicine.

To the descendants, and to the memory of
Flash Silvermoon

✴

Thank you, Pecan Tree, keeper of my shade on Summit Drive, and Fireflies, my night companions under Pappy's windowsill.

Thank you, Rob, for always being real.

Thank you, Stephanie and Marsha, for being the most wonderful commas I could have asked for, when I needed them most,

Natalie, I'm so grateful for you. Every step, every word, all the wyrd.

Thanks to the staff at Inner Traditions, particularly Meghan MacLean, Jon Graham, and Erica Robinson for your support and spirit in shaping this book.

Contents

The Problem of Animism

Animism is the experience that everything has consciousness, that the world is made up of persons, some human, and some not.[1] In that awareness everything is in relationship, communicating, impacting, and interacting on various levels of agency. There is no individual; thus the emphasis is on right relationship, community. Within that interaction lies the responsibility for how we affect where we literally stand and the greater relationship to All Things.

When I teach animism to students, they don't understand what it is at first. They struggle to locate themselves through awareness, embodiment, grounding, and experience *only*. They can't hold themselves as part of Nature. They struggle with the reflex to intellectualize animism, to reduce it merely to science or mysticism, and as a result, they compartmentalize it to our ancient past or to specific present cultural groups, regions, or species they (unconsciously) consider to be less sophisticated. Each of these projections carries a deep bias that reveals our own traumatic histories of oppressed and oppressor, which serve to separate us not only from our animistic roots but from our animistic potential. These biases reinforce settler culture, which is a power structure built on the displacement and exploitation of indigenous people and their culture by an invading immigrant culture, and contributes to the need to see ourselves as separate from each other, Nature, and the spirit world.

I point out that we aren't just *part* of Nature, we *are* Nature. Our words *earth* and *human* are etymologically related through Latin via the Proto-Indo-European origin word, *dʰéǵʰōm*, which means "earth" or "soil."[2] *We are where we stand.*

We discuss how animism doesn't just exist in the rear-view mirror of humanity. It's also in our cradles and baby dolls, as we're all born animists. We're all born aware that everything is alive and that we're continually in direct relationship with it. As children, we feel that trees are family. We talk to them and listen for a response. Our stuffed animals and invisible friends sit at the dinner table.

It's only when we reach puberty that settler culture demands we leave the childishness of the liminal behind, that we devalue it for the sake of collective intellectual advancement, that we exploit kin resources to our benefit, and that we fashion our psyches into something more useful for systemic productivity. By adolescence we realize that even in our rebellions against settler culture, we've been groomed for the separation from Self as Nature all along. For that matter, in many ways we have benefited from that separation—some of us more than others. I point out that all of this complication aside, we're all *still* animists because we aren't separate from anything. We never have been.

Rune Hjarnø Rasmussen, Ph.D., says, "In cultures with strong animist knowledge, animism is something you take a lifetime to learn. Elders are the ones that know it the best, not children."[3] Settler culture has ripped such knowledge from us. Instead we're taught to invalidate the animistic paths of indigenous people and our Ancestors, the pure connectedness of our children, and our own direct experience, and we don't have elders who retain and pass on legacies of animistic wisdom to us. We may be innate animists, but we aren't eldering well with it. We have not approached eldering as a lifelong practice that deepens with knowledge and wisdom.

When we speak of *elders* and *elderhood*, it isn't a matter of age. Rather, we are referring to those people in our communities who are trusted and respected for the knowledge and wisdom they have gained through their lived experience and their ability to apply that understanding to educate, support, and sustain the community. Once upon a time that understanding included animistic wisdom. Sadly, it is in short supply today.

When we sit with the multiple rejections of our kinship with Nature, we're left to investigate why. I explain to my students that this lack of connection is the broken path, the forced fracture of our relationship to Nature, from our ancient land-based wisdom, and in the gap of that brokenness is every cultural wound we experience. It is the heart of our disconnection from and devaluing of each other. It is the colonized projection of the individual, which justifies taking no responsibility for relationship. It is our inability to make the connection between the agency of our toaster, our cousin, and consumerism. It is our traumatic separation from the wisdom of our Ancestors and the disrespect of elders and descendants. It is the advent of trauma itself. It is why we can't function without modern conveniences even while sitting with the harm they create. It is why we don't know how to survive in the wild. When we sit with these rejections we also find little to no space held for our Sacred Selves. When we can't locate our sacredness in that gap, we realize that our settler-centric systems and institutions intentionally propagate the brokenness, and our unconscious biases as folx raised in those systems set us up to, in turn, unconsciously exacerbate the wound.*

I tell them that until we make these biases conscious, our best efforts are still breaking the path. Until our models of care include all bone, soil, water, air, and fungi, we're still breaking the path. After the shock, denial, grief, and humiliation, their heartbreak around that realization and commitment to tending the spirited path gives way to the ancient call of the wild: embody, be, do.

We confront that we've always been animists without awareness or intention. As they settle into a fraught relationship with Nature, we discuss that by using the word *animism* to describe earth kinship, we've already reduced thousands of years of tradition and compressed

---

*The spelling of *folx* rather than *folks* is used intentionally to indicate gender inclusivity.

the organic ways of being of countless peoples into one academic word that was never intended to truly describe any of this with respect. We begin to understand that the experience we call animism existed before words. Yet as is so often the case with English, it's the word we have. It's a word indigenous people don't use and in many cases don't accept as an appropriate or worthy descriptor of their all-kin traditions, juxtaposed with the efforts of scholars like Graham Harvey to reclaim it from a derogatory or critical term, and convey that there are as many animisms as there are cultures.[4]

Life choices change. Everything becomes sacred. Lineages reconcile. Communities thrive. We become more interested in verbs than nouns, tending rather than healing or curing. We realize that we are not just in relationship with Nature, but as indigenous poet, musician, and public speaker Lyla June, Ph.D., says, we are family with Nature and All Things.[5] We realize that we are Nature. We begin knowing that animism is place-based experience of relationship. Only when we tend the broken path through eldering ourselves into direct relationship with All Things and surrender to the experience, knowledge, and wisdom of that bond do we understand ourselves as elders. Only when we embody and educate ourselves as animists do we create new paths worthy of our descendants and help facilitate healthy community for all peoples. And only when we understand that any iteration of animism we live in this time will still be incomplete do we begin to understand who we are becoming and what regenerative possibilities we can concoct. Our creative capacity, agency, and gratitude are the unique alchemy human persons bring to the planet, and they know no bounds.

I can identify with these biased responses in my students, understand where they're coming from, and hold space for where they can go because I had those responses, too. I am a white, disabled, neurologically other, nonbinary, pansexual, female-bodied person who carries a certain marginalization along with privilege in settler culture. I still work through layers of blindness with regard to Nature, denial, bias, authority (my own and that of others), normalcy, and care. I still feel into the yearning of missing roots and draw out fear, awe, power, grief, hatred, and joy. I grew up with a grandfather who taught me that everything around me was alive and that my actions affect us all, and I still struggle to internalize what that really means in how I move among the relationships of this world. And I do very specifically say "move among" because as animists we don't move "through," or even "with." We are not isolated flesh-bound objects distinct from place. We are place made flesh. *We move among, connected with and carrying all of life, always in relationship, moving with us.* I continue to learn how I need to move among differently, so that I honor all life, every day. All things considered, this book is not my success story, but one step in my elderhood. It is *one* route to doing better, of which there are infinite options.

Much of soul-tending discourse is now devoted to reaching into the deep past of *well Ancestors*—or those who have moved on from the living realm, reconciled their personal and collective traumas, and returned to oneness and are now ancestral Spirit Allies—and asking them to walk with us through these difficult times. Yet we don't talk as much about our *hungry ghosts*—an ancient Asian reference to unreconciled dead, who feed on the life force of the living—or emphasize how we, ourselves, become well Ancestors. In this omission, we still aren't addressing how we got here, or where fit elderhood is situated in not only how we live but how we die as well. Those things are related.

As well, we are not properly acknowledging that despite being conscripted into settler culture, indigenous cultures do have unbroken elder-Nature relationships that go back thousands of years, and that fact doesn't grant outsiders rights to their wisdom and teachings. We aren't appropriately acknowledging that others who were forced into settler culture forged supportive relationship with the indigenous people, ecosystems, and nonhuman spirits here, without taking. They made new paths where they stood.

As outsiders in place, we need to tend and cultivate our own way, a process that can only be accomplished by sitting with the brokenness, the histories of oppressed, oppressor, and supremacy, retrieving the strengths and wisdom of our lines and adapting teachings from those experiences to meet the needs of our time. In short, we have to deal with our shit without pathologizing it and from that wisdom cultivate strong lore in place that outlives us.

In settler culture we are broken from awareness of our inherent family in Nature, as are we broken from rites rooted in place and elements that create of us fit elders. Only when we realize that the break is recent, that for thousands of years we thoroughly engaged animistic eldering skills and situated ourselves healthily and intentionally into direct relationship with All Things, do we begin to feel that doing so again is possible.

This is eldering well, and it is within our reach. We can hold the wisdom and wounds of our Ancestors, as well as the liminal landscapes of our childhood, so that they lead us into better relationship with ourselves, Nature, our communities, and the spirit world. Through revisiting and creating vital aspects of life initiation, we on the broken path can create possible ways to get there. These include the following:

- Understanding our *actual* relationship to Nature rather than one we borrow, project, or romanticize
- Owning our personal role in the broken path and its impact on All Things
- Forming and continuously tending a cosmology through engaging the resources available at all levels to reconcile our disruption from kinship with Nature, the spirit world, our Ancestors, and the pool of living elder wisdom and recognizing the protection this brings
- Allowing the emergence of our Sacred Self through the rite of heartbreak
- Learning to embody and ground our sacredness for collective wholeness
- Tracing and reconciling life patterns that perpetuate the collective break
- Honoring our calling to tend community through discovering our personal relationship with All Things

- Passing on our wisdom with compassion by valuing our unique gift enough to give it
- Standing in the danger of the harm we've caused by engaging the relationship between agency and impact

By engaging these steps of growth and initiation and working through the personal introspection and engagement provoked by this book, we can cultivate our unique way to elder well. Each chapter includes introspections that use experiential exercises and journaling to come more into direct relationship with what eldering well really means. For some of the exercises, it would be helpful to have the skill to induce an intentional trance, but it isn't required.

To truly engage this material and build the foundation needed to support the initiations of eldering well, approach it slowly and thoroughly. Take your time as you read through it all, and be sure to complete each introspection before progressing to the next chapter. Initiation into elderhood is the work of our lives, much of which in specificity is well beyond the scope of this book.

To clarify, this book doesn't take you through a linear step-by-step approach to elderhood. That isn't possible to orchestrate in a meaningful way. Rather, it celebrates our unique paths, cosmologies, and rituals and describes the dynamics that affect how we hold our agency and with which we are in relationship, so that we can each bring them into our awareness of eldering in our own way.

No one will become a fit elder just from reading this book; I'm not one just for writing it. This book was not written out of mastery but out of a longing for something I have not had, something that hasn't been available in broken-path settler culture. This book doesn't teach you how to be a fit elder, but it introduces components of eldering well that can start you on an animistic path.

That path will require self-awareness within relationship, skills, compassionate curiosity, and follow-through with each of these components to grow into our unique role as elder. My highest hope is that it sparks further exploration to express personal separation from Nature in a cultural context; to understand that Nature is All Things—all human and nonhuman beings and spirits; to see Self as inseparable from ecosystem; to find and cultivate power in relationship with Nature; to experience the connection between elderhood and Nature; to gain potential to see Self as elder, standing between the Ancestors and the descendants; and as much as possible to set life up in a way that supports our fit elderhood.

In truth, the path of our inherent relationship with Nature isn't and has never been *broken*; we have only been locked in the cultural perception of not experiencing it. We've unconsciously participated in the lie that by virtue of being human we were always separate from and better than Nature. We have unknowingly participated in the lie that because we ancestrally created this mess and have perpetuated it through our own wounding, it must also be our final destiny. We have been groomed to ignore the path, to ignore our own wounding around separation from it, and to ignore that a path that leads into our ancestral kinship and land relationship still exists. The apathy generated from this systemic gaslighting is the indescribable yearning for something more that is so arrested by wounding it conveys like we don't care, when in reality we care immensely and feel cut off from our sources of power to tend those wounds. From within those wounds, such kinship is ours to cultivate and tend, and the capability of that lived experience is wholly before us. Such is our origin of trauma and the route to fit elderhood.

Where that exploration leads us requires that we not only be detached from the outcome but that we prepare ourselves for not living to see its full manifestation. In fact, part of eldering well means that we won't be around to see the outcome of our work here. Still, once we know it's possible to be a fit elder, once we feel connected to a new way of being, we realize that we're not alone in this pursuit, and that through awareness of relationship with Nature, we can create new paths to elderhood that sustain. In this way, we outcreate the system. We make new paths.

INTROSPECTION

Identifying Your Dream Team

The topics covered in this book will bring up big feelings. To give them the healthy expression they require, it will be helpful to identify and engage your support community—those human persons you can call on for help in all areas of your life. I call this community your Dream Team, and in every class that I teach (and in my books), I encourage folx to organize their Dream Team *prior* to beginning study. Because I don't have the range to teach every skill I note in this book, I point to many resources to help you process what comes up. But even with those possibilities in place, assess your own Dream Team to help you fill needs that arise as you do the work of this book. Commit to exploring these anchors as you process your personal experience of the broken path and animism, and expect your Dream Team to change as you do.

Consider which spirit or earthly beings you would go to for support in each of the following categories:

* Emotional
* Psychological
* Physical
* Medical (allopathic and holistic)
* Nutritional
* Spiritual
* Energetic
* Basic needs
* Financial
* Gender
* Religious
* Antioppression
* Sexuality
* Identity
* Crisis
* Accountability
* Reparation
* Witnessing
* Transformative justice

Exploring Your Relationships with Nature and Community

A secondary reason for organizing your Dream Team is that community is the whole point of animism. It is the ability to manage relationships well, which entails knowing your resources, calling on them when needed, feeding them when they need it, and continuously tending that entire support cycle.

As you cultivate a direct relationship with your Dream Team and the broken path, I strongly encourage you to journal on the following:

✻ What immediately comes to mind when you think of animism?

✻ What aspects of your life feel threatened by living more animistically?

✻ What are you willing to risk to embody yourself and move through life as an animist? As an elder?

✻ Are you willing to embody a way of moving among that isn't here yet?

✻ What is most frightening to you about living animistically?

✻ What is most frightening to you about embracing elderhood?

✻ What do you perceive as the cost of not doing so?

✻ How does your body respond when you allow yourself to feel relationship to the broken path?

✻ Your body has never felt distanced from Nature. When you sit with that awareness, what does your body communicate?

✻ How can you support and respond to those feelings in a healthy way?

✻ When you think of family, what sensations come up in your body? How comfortable are you with these feelings?

✻ How comfortable are you with the human persons in your life whom you consider family?

✻ How comfortable are you with the human persons in your life whom you don't consider family?

✻ Consider how any complex feelings will affect your family relationship to Nature.

✻ Consider this question: Have we always been animists but simply unaware of it?

1

Our Cultural Relationship to Animistic Elderhood

Owning Our Personal Role in the Broken Path

There's no desire to be an adult. Adulthood is not a goal. It's not seen as a gift. Something happened culturally: No one is supposed to age past 45—sartorially, cosmetically, attitudinally.

FRANCES MCDORMAND,
"A STAR WHO HAS NO TIME FOR VANITY"

A word I see coming up often in social contexts is *adulting*, as in, "I washed the laundry and voted, today. *I adulted*." As if the step from child to adult and all it entails is extra. As if only certain people are expected to mature. As if we all carry the same expectations, time frame, privilege, and projections around what adulthood means. Instead of furthering those projections, I go with a verb I feel encompasses the experience better—*humaning*—as it reflects the range of responsibility, growth, and maturity demanded by life through *all* stages of development. Humaning reflects a process. At four years old, we can human well through personal action that benefits the family by taking our own dirty dishes to the sink. At forty years old we can human well by tithing and volunteering to benefit the community. At eighty years old we can human well by sharing with our descendants what worked and what didn't, what we know now and wish we'd known then.

At heart, humaning well is something we all strive for and is expected of us, but humaning is hard. How do we get there? How do we human well? What resources and skills must we have to become that healthy balanced being? And why haven't we had them? The truth is, the term *adulting* isn't born from a rejection of maturity or a lazy attitude. It stems from the fatigue of generations who have been forced into an artificial projection of what adulthood should look like without the opportunity to arrive at an organic version of it and without the emotional, psychological, and spiritual tools they need to truly succeed at *any* version of it.

Our best resource for such growth is our elders, though therein lies one of our greatest cultural lacks. Our elders are the keepers of lore, which is the bridge between us and our Ancestors, the spirit world, and myth. According to Dictionary.com, a myth is "a traditional story, especially one concerning the early history of a people or explaining some natural or social phenomenon, and typically involving supernatural beings or events." Myth is the animistic component of lore, the magickal aspect of the human narrative that reminds us we are Divine. Where we read about what seems to be impossible or absurd in mythology, we can decode it as being the representation of the Divine, the Sacred, the unseen animistic.

Likewise, lore is "a body of traditions and knowledge on a subject or held by a particular group, typically passed from person to person by word of mouth." This knowledge is tradition-encompassing learned information passed to new generations. Lore involves stories, data about human-wildlife relationship, documentation of the path of communities through time and circumstance, and the myths that evolved as part of that narrative.

From an animistic standpoint, lore comprises cosmologies and relationships that help us make sense of the multiverse, our place in it, and our place in our communities. Cosmology is an assessment of how life as we understand it happens and the key forces that play a role in how life evolves and how it works.

The animistic mechanisms on Earth and in spirit—including the elements, directions, science, Spirit Allies, aspects of Self, human-persons community, tools (such as oracles, sacred texts, and rituals), Ancestors, and other meaningful components—make up a living, evolving connection between us and the spirit world that we access and engage in our spiritual practice through various means. That connection provides us with the lens through which we assess how we're moving through life and see ourselves in All Things and find them within ourselves. In short, this connection is our cosmology, which is the container of our relationships.

Through lore, cosmology conveys literal evidence of how we fit into life, mythologized with spiritual meaning for how we move among, as well as instruction for how to stay in evolving relationship with cosmology that has been deemed worthy enough to pass on to descendants.

Inherited lore informs how we create and sustain relationships to Nature, Spirit Allies, ourselves, and our communities. We all have the capability to human well throughout life, as we all have the capability to elder well through our life's wisdom. What remains in question is how we create the systems, structures, skills, and supports for us to all access our deepest capability to actually do so, when we haven't had true elders to show us how.

And by that I don't mean everything is our parents' fault. When I say we have a cultural lack of animistic elders, I mean our experience of the broken path has created us as a people without a relationship to true eldering. In reality, our parents didn't have fit animistic elders, and neither did their parents, and so on as far back as a few thousand years. In my estimation, and as I craft a potential for eldering well in this book, we lost our direct ties to eldering well when our indigeneity was absorbed into an overculture, when we were removed from Nature, when we stopped being animists, when we became colonized. The lack of well animistic elders is old, but in the grander scheme of being, it is not ancient. It is not who we always were.

When we sit with the realization that our Ancestors had a more intact direct relationship to Nature, we have to explore what caused our break from it. The specific catalysts are different in different parts of the world, and I can only speak to the one that I'm ancestrally connected to: the destabilization of indigenous Europe. As my ancestry and cosmology are comprised of Old Norse figures and concepts, occasionally in the text I refer to Old Norse terms. It is wholly appropriate to determine for yourself whether those or similar concepts are relevant to your ancestry and cosmology, and if so, how you might engage them through the reading of this book.

In her book *The Norse Shaman*, Evelyn Rysdyk presents a cohesive narrative of natural factors that contributed to the changed European/Eurasian relationship to Nature. The literal lay of the land changed with the extreme rise and fall of the sea level, which affected access to ancestral lands. With these shifts in terrain and access, famine forced an adaptation of skills. The relationship to land relied fully on elders' knowledge of migration patterns and seasonal resources to survive. As Rysdyk points out, the most vulnerable of these populations wouldn't have survived the catastrophic flooding that ensued, with the foremost among the losses being elders. Without their wisdom the entire community would have been at higher risk of collapse.[1] After generations of success as hunter-gatherers on vast familiar lands, rapid climate change forced folx to shift to farming in order to sustain their food supplies, which also meant becoming less nomadic.

It's difficult to convey in a few sentences the disruption, despair, and trauma that would have resulted from such a huge life change in a relatively short period of time. To give it better context, Gabor Maté has done extensive work distinguishing what we would consider a painful occurrence from that of trauma. In the documentary *The Wisdom of Trauma*, Maté stated, "Children don't get traumatized because they're hurt. They get traumatized because they're alone with the hurt."[2] They experience trauma because the fullness of their experience of pain is not held in community. Given this, pain becomes trauma when we're not witnessed and brought back to a sense of Self that is indistinguishable from community. Pain becomes trauma when it is not held in Oneness. The same could be said of entire peoples, of the cultural disruption of our Ancestors. When they lost a sense of personal and cultural wholeness along with their kinship with Nature, *then* pain became trauma. The transition and its aftermath would have compounded into a direct impact on sacred rituals, Nature relationships, and surviving elders. It would have created division, such that people would have been pitted against each other for resources and power in a way they never had been before. It would have created isolation that became trauma.

While climate change altered our relationship to each other and Nature through lost access to ancestral lands, the shift to farming, and the loss of elders, a more intentional and systemic factor took that broken path to new levels. The acquisition of power in the hands of a few through amassing large tracts of land that were once held in common by the people became a tactic of colonization, imperialism, and the church. According to historian Bettany Hughes, "Christianity appeared on a planet that had been, for at least 70,000 years, animist."[3] The end of this span of thriving as animists in North and South America and most of Europe coincides with the growing force of Christian colonization. This time frame means that we were animists until around the last four to five thousand years. It seems like a long time to have amassed a lot of damage and lost valuable lore, but over seventy thousand years is a long time to cultivate many well Ancestors. These spirit allies lived a human-person experience of hardship, interdependence, Nature kinship, and belonging, and they are our best resources in learning to elder well.

In the time frame that the church became dominant, animistic traditions across the globe were at best conscripted into Christian rubric and at worst were lost forever. For most, survival would have meant aligning with the most successful power structure. How the church enforced this power structure was most telling, with regard to animism. The foremost animistic detriment in colonization was the forced removal of peoples from their sacred lands or being enslaved to work them.

This change in relationship to land also resulted in a change in identity. This is the point that many European cultures shifted from land-based identity to blood-based ancestry, which divested us from Nature kinship. In *The Sacred Flame* podcast, host Mathias Nordvig states, "The old practice of caring for and about your land-based Ancestors that existed before the conversion to Christianity was stripped of its numinous and ritual context to simply become the practice of carrying a name of distinction that was inherited through blood relations."[4]

But of course blood-based ancestry was to the detriment of those who were not wealthy. Violence toward land is always violence toward human persons, an association that is still true today in the fight for indigenous land and water preservation in the Americas.[5]

This violence began in the form of laws made by the church forbidding direct relationship to Nature. In *The Book of Seidr*, Runic John outlines many of these disruptions in tribal Europe. Here are a few examples:

Xtian* Laws (690 CE)

If anyone makes or performs a vow at trees, springs, or stones or boundaries or anywhere other than the house of God, let him do penance of three years . . .

The Laws of King Edgar (959–975 CE)

And we enjoin that every priest zealously promote xtianity* and totally extinguish aver Heathenism; and forbid well worshipping

---

*The original text uses *xtian* and *xtianity*, meaning Christian/Christianity

and spiritualism and divination and enchantments and idol worshipping and the vain practices which are carried out with various
spells and peace-enclosure (Frithgarth) and with elders and with
various other trees and with stones and with many various delusions
with which men do much of what they should not.

The Laws of King Canut (1020–1023 CE)

And we earnestly forbid any Heathenism. Heathenism is that men
worship idols, that is they worship the Heathen gods, and the sun
and moon, fire or rivers, water, well or stone or forest tree of any
kind or love witchcraft or promote deathwork in any wise or by sac-
rifice or by divination do pertain to such illusions.[6]

These are just a few examples of the laws that were passed and the
punishments that were meted out for direct engagement with Nature
and the spirit world. When we look at these punishments not just as
static acts from the past but as violent traumas inflicted on our animistic Ancestors that we have brought forward in laws, social and cultural
marginalization, unconscious biases, intergenerational trauma, and well-
intended spiritual practices, we see how we aren't just continuing to play
out these separations, we are actually complicit in sustaining our separation from Nature and the spirit world. We could even go as far as to
say that until the break from our awareness of our kinship with Nature,
trauma didn't exist. Until we were leveraged away from the experience
of wholeness and all of the relationships that included, it didn't need to.

These historic laws were Manifest Destiny 1.0, and they began
the slow methodical, systemic colonization of people and land by the
church. These European edicts were the foundation of legalized othering that spanned the world, based on gender, ethnicity, sexual orienta-
tion, disability, age, spirituality, and so on. Specifically, these laws didn't
just facilitate the loss of European indigenous kinship with Nature,
they facilitated the erasure of all people who embraced that kinship.
In the 1400s the church created the concept of "terra nullius," or

no-man's-land, under the Doctrine of Discovery, implying that land not occupied by Christians was up for grabs, and through the subjugation and enslavement of indigenous peoples, lands were taken. The Doctrine of Discovery is still used to justify the taking of indigenous land today.[7]

Again, violence toward land is violence toward human persons. These laws remain part of our unconscious justification that our right to destroy natural resources nullifies our responsibility for the harm that comes to the people who protect them. The decimation of traditional cultures around the world was the decimation of the relationship between human persons and Nature, of animism, and it still is.

Because this violence is still perpetuated—particularly against indigenous people and people of color—those of us intentionally reclaiming our animacy cannot arrive at a personal relationship to it without also reconciling how the present state of the human-Nature relationship came to be through our Ancestors and how we currently situate with privilege in the systems that replaced animism, as well as supporting the peoples who have protected the land and preserved that relationship at great cost all these centuries—even to today.

These laws are also why we culturally don't acknowledge human persons as part of Nature, or other-than-human spirits as "alive." They serve as the basis for seeing animals, plants, elements, and so on as lesser beings. Are humans kin to Nature? Yes. Are all beings consciousness with agency? Yes, though we have not cultivated the perception that we are or live through it in our daily lives. When we can't see ourselves as kin to Nature or envision all beings as valuable and as having agency, we can't create direct relationship with them, we can't protect them or ourselves.

The absence of such an intimate land relationship is why settler culture descendants have few remnants of ancient rituals for honoring the land or knowledge of our ancestral origins. Ritual and ceremony are the spiritual technologies that create lore, and without them, lore is lost. Author Steven Farmer, Ph.D., has a specific distinction in mind when he describes these technologies. According to him, "Ritual is something that we do in order to call upon or beseech the forces of creation to act on our behalf. Ceremony is the inspired expression of our dance with creation."[8]

As animists, applying these tools allows us to *intentionally* bridge the everyday with the Divine for some purpose. They allow human persons to create, sustain, and engage safe space—a boundary in which sacred work is done. In that safe container, through ritual and ceremony, we engage cosmology. In this way, relationship with a thriving, healthy cosmology provides strong guidance for how to cultivate ourselves as elders.

Ritual, ceremony, and cosmology are the means through which we form and develop direct relationship to the actual land, its spiritual aspects and inhabitants, our Ancestors, aspects of ourselves, our communities, and our planet. When rituals and ceremonies are disrupted, direct relationships and cosmologies can't support us. When we become distanced from those relationships and cosmologies, we lose our lore.

In addition to disconnecting us from ritual and lore, historic laws also separated us from sacred burial sites, and thus deathwalking rituals, which is why so many dead remain unreconciled and contribute to intergenerational trauma. In fact, these rituals likely would have included spiritual technologies that would have prevented pain from becoming trauma—technologies we are only just now widely reclaiming in how we move among.

The toll of these disruptions to Spirits of Place (the unique, regional nonhuman spirits) has affected the human trajectory on the planet, and it affects us still, in our daily lives. When human persons aren't engaging in their rituals to reconcile their pain, that pain becomes trauma. And if trauma is not reconciled, the dead can't move on from the earthly realm. They remain here, as do their wounds, to be felt and played out repeatedly by the living.

Thus, disrupting the intimate relationship with the land also affects the spirit world. When the dead aren't given rites that effectively move them out of the human domain, reconcile their personal life and ancestral trauma, and position them to freely and confidently move on to What Comes Next, aspects of sacred order are disrupted. Folx who don't move on don't become well Ancestors, and without them, we lose support on the human level to generate necessary change. As with all in relationship—even the unquiet dead—a destructive cycle is set up that affects all of life when they don't move on.

The glaring truth behind all of this is that once our European Ancestors were colonized, they turned that trauma into colonizing other cultures. They set a trauma pattern into motion that not only denied and compounded their indigeneity and experience of colonization but also created additional trauma for themselves and others by doing to others what was done to them. In the same way that early ancestral laws of displacement formed the basis of institutional othering that biases our socioeconomic and political systems today, the behavioral responses of our Ancestors formed the attitudes, fear, and hatred that currently empower othering. This destructive part of our past isn't separate from our culture of hatred now. It is not separate from our collective and personal perceptions of being broken from Nature.

We can't stop climate change and natural disasters that could affect us in much the same way they did our Ancestors. But we can protect land and resources and by doing so possibly prevent further disaster. We can open ourselves to experiencing the world around us not just as beings with consciousness but potentially as family with whom we share an interwoven well-being. We can directly provide support to the human persons and organizations that protect Nature. We can improve the overall quality of life for all beings by supporting leaders and policy that give everyone access to fair emergency support, clean water, nutritive food, safe shelter, education, medical care, and mental and emotional support. These acts are all doable ways to tend the broken path and reforge animistic connection, though they require close examination of personal habits and internal patterning for them to be effective.

We can't change old, intentionally harmful systems that are now autonomous life forces fighting to survive, but we can assess how we each break the path through our day-to-day choices, which inadvertently support those harmful systems. We can cultivate an awareness of which choices we can make differently, which ones we can't, and the influences that control what our options are, and we can tend the spiritual ramifications and roots of all of the aforementioned. No, we can't just mind over matter colonization and thousands of years of supremacy. But we can examine where in the existing systems we hold privilege and use it to improve the life circumstances of those more vulnerable to erratic life change and harmful systems. We can listen to those who know better and already know how to exact positive change.

In this way, how we approach our direct relationship to Nature is interwoven with our attitudes toward racism, poverty, capitalism, disability, misogyny, body shaming, colonization, queerphobia, transphobia, xenophobia, and all manner of othering systems. As we come more into our personal power and awareness, we can evoke change to benefit our communities. We can speak out and hold accountable those who have more power than we do to initiate change on a bigger scale.

When we elder a sustainable way of being for all persons, human and other-than-human, we open new pathways for us all. We begin to shape new lore based on shared cosmologies that become their own life force (or already were), to grow new roots that support us and our descendants. When we heal the thread that connects our wisdom to lore, we begin to see ourselves as elders.

Let's get started.

INTROSPECTION

Exploring Your Personal Relationship with the Broken Path

This chapter describes our collective relationship to the broken path, though we must also explore our personal relationship to it.

Take some time to do just that. Engaging the broken path's spiritual manifestation—visiting its spirit—may give you a better feel for where you situate on it and what tending that relationship needs at this time. It may be that this dialogue comes through Nature engagement, your body, or a dream. It may come through an intentionally induced trance state. How it comes isn't as important as setting the intention to find it in your life and hold space for it to come. In this very intimate way, you can gain a felt sense of its journey, how it shows up in your personal life, how it shows up collectively, and how you can embody your role with it as an elder.

In a safe, quiet space, verify that this work is right for you to pursue at this time. If it isn't, consult the part(s) of you that voices concern and work with your Spirit Allies to address that concern. As you cultivate direct relationship with the broken path, I heavily encourage you to journal on the following:

✳ Describe your encounter(s) with the spirit of the broken path. How did meeting that spirit impact your feelings about them? How do you carry that experience forward in everyday actions?

✳ As you explore your feelings and attitude toward the broken path, consider your relationship to Nature, climate change, plants, elements, animals, resources that you consume, trauma, other human persons, yourself. What do your feelings about these aspects have in common? Where do they differ?

✳ Explore your feelings and attitude toward the broken path alongside racism, misogyny, queerphobia, transphobia, xenophobia, poverty, capitalism, disability, body shaming, colonization, capitalism, and all othering you can imagine. What do your feelings about these aspects have in common? Where do they differ?

✳ How have you benefited from the broken path? Name the systems that you most benefit from, such as the banking, education, or medical systems or even more general systems like capitalism, democracy, or social mobility.

❈ How have you been marginalized by it? Name the systems that most marginalize you.

❈ What privileges do you hold that specifically reinforce the break (i.e., take power from others)?

❈ How have you resisted reconciliation of the break despite understanding the harm it's created?

❈ Where in that break have you found growth?

❈ When you sit with your direct relationship to the break, what feelings are brought up?

❈ How do you educate yourself about life among in a way that doesn't demand that education from indigenous people or appropriate their traditions?

❈ What people, communities, and systems in your immediate life contributed to your trauma of the break?

❈ How do you sustain relationship with them and mend your part of the path?

❈ What is your ancestral relationship to this break?

❈ Are your Spirit Allies aware of the broken path? Have you talked with them about it?

❈ How do you reconcile being an animist in a capitalist culture?

Exploring Your Personal Relationship with Ecosystem Kin

Take some time to explore the space where you live—indoors and out—where possible. Learn who lives with you in your ecosystem. Ecosystem kin, or Naturekin, comprise many beings. They are animals, trees, or specific areas in the grass, though they can also be elements, elementals, directions, structures (even specific rooms or materials used in the structures), specific mountains or formations (even clouds), Land Elders (my term for human spirits who have stayed after death to hold part of the human-Nature relationship), Ancestors, Spirits of Place, celestial parents (Earth and Sky) and so on.

Explore your relationship to these places and beings by considering the following:

❋ What other humans occupy your home, neighborhood, region, communities, and so on with you? Describe your relationship to them, including how you meet each other's needs and possibly where you don't.

❋ Where does your body stop and start in your immediate ecosystem kinships?

❋ Where does possession of your body start and stop with microbes and bacteria?

❋ What's your climate like?

❋ What's your relationship to seasonality?

❋ What in your place-space changes with the seasons?

❋ What in your body or mind changes with the seasons?

❋ What animals, plants, trees, stones, bodies of water, and so forth live there? Describe your relationship with them, including how you meet each other's needs.

❋ What Spirits of Place do you sense?

❋ What elements do you work with in your spiritual path?

❋ How do the directions situate in your spiritual path?

❋ What Naturekin walk with you?

❋ What relationship exists between the elements, directions, Nature Allies, and yourself?

❋ How are you in reciprocity with all of the above?

❋ What in your life needs mythologizing so that you can build better lore?

❋ How does your trauma show up in the Naturekin around you?

❋ How does the trauma of your ecosystem show up in your body? Your life?

2
Repairing the Human-Nature Relationship

Engaging the Resources to Reconcile Our Separation from Nature

In order to build the movements capable of transforming our world, we have to do our best to live with one foot in the world we have not yet created.

AURORA LEVINS MORALES,
"A REVOLUTION CAPABLE OF HEALING OUR WOUNDS"

We're not supposed to have to hold our space alone. By "space" I mean our energetic hygiene, protection, boundaries, health, balance—all of it. We're not supposed to *have* to do it alone. In fact, we don't do it alone.

Read that phrase again: we don't do it alone. It's a strange concept isn't it? After a lifetime of having individuality shoved down our throats, our value is based on how well we function alone, professionally, socially, mentally, and financially, and we so heavily enforce individualism that we see reliance on community as weak or flawed. Likewise, we project the idea that community has little to no responsibility for its people.[1]

Such is the revolutionary thinking of settler culture Americans. In truth, human persons are collections of relationships, dynamics, ecosystems that are always evolving. There is no such thing as individual.

So who is supposed to help us hold our space? All humans in collective agreement? Sure. Human persons are built for relationship. We are meant to thrive in healthy community. To that end, we all play a role in how well we're all doing at any given time, whether we're consciously aware of that fact or we aren't. Sadly, however, we don't collectively agree that we're all looking out for each other. And for the record, community is the one thing that clients and students most often tell me they don't have on their animistic paths. Lacking community is a big part of the broken path. Assuming that other human persons are supposed to help us hold our space, we have some work to do there.

Will Spirit Allies and Helpers hold our space? Sort of, though from my perspective that's not really their job, or at least not in the earth-rooted way I'm referring to here. I know some folx have different views on that. In the 1990s New Age guru era, everything was all about Spirit Guides. They were the new saviors put forward as the one-stop shop for every request: soulmate, prosperity, health . . . done. The thing is, most Spirit Helpers don't know crap about earthly life. They don't know what it's like to human because most of them have never lived a human-person experience, or if they have, it was likely in a radically different time. That is what distinguishes them from Naturekin and Ancestors. Most Spirit Allies don't have direct knowledge of life in form. They are very detached from the ordeal of humaning, by design. Their job is to hold the space of the playing field for us to create within. In other words, Spirit Allies tend the arena in which we keep the balls in the air, but they don't directly control any of it; they just hold the space. We choose which balls to toss, what colors they're painted, how they spin, and whether the field is natural grass or turf.

Spirit Helpers do cheerlead us in our effort, but if they became entrenched in the passionate, emotional workings of earthly life (and some do), they wouldn't have the detachment necessary to hold the space. They don't have humans' heart and passion, which are required to generate change here. Yes, they can inspire us, even enlighten us. But it is our job to do something with that inspiration. *Doing* is how we reciprocate their inspiration. Part of coming into form is submitting to the rules of the arena. We become the game mentally, emotionally, physically. We channel our spiritual agency into creating life while we're here.

I experience Spirit Allies less as all-inclusive helpers of the human-person experience and more as background supporters who are always present but situationally helpful, given permission and good boundaries. To me, they are the idea persons and we are the implementation persons. They hold the space for the thoughtform in Other, the spirit realm, so that we can build it in form here on Earth. Both roles are required, though the heavy lifting in form rests solely on humanity. When we aren't on top of our implementation game and are waiting for our Spirit Allies to just shazam something into being for us, our relationship to them becomes compromised. It becomes one-sided and eventually burns out. That we have leaned on Spirit Helpers for every little play to accomplish that creation into form has resulted in a gross imbalance of power and is partly why we have a broken path to our well Ancestors, their lands, and their rituals.

How about Nature Spirits? First of all, who are they? Not knowing who Nature Spirits are is in part why the path is broken. For me they are Naturekin, other-than-human spirits who are most engaged at the earth-elemental level (as opposed to ones that are mostly engaged at other levels, such as Spirit Allies, deities, thoughtforms, or oracle spirits, for example). In Old Norse cosmology, they are called *wights* or *landvaettir*. They can be the souls of trees, air, grass, barred owls, sidewalks, ponds, kitchens (*husvaettir*, or house spirits), or whole regions.

When Nature Spirits come up in the conversation of human persons holding space, it's usually in the context of grounding, as in, "Being barefoot in the grass brings me back in my body," "Hugging trees helps me feel connected," or "Amethyst is an ally for me." The thing about "grounding yourself in Nature" is that Nature isn't really invested in our "grounding"—or at least not in a "humans are special" sort of way. I mean, as we are family of Nature, Nature wants us to be well. Nature perceives humanity as part of themself. It isn't possible for Nature to conceive of themself as anything but a whole community or of tending to that community as anything but sacred order. To that end, Nature wants to play a role in facilitating us in doing what we came here to do. The cultivation of our creative capabilities and how we can engage matter to produce change is a miracle of Nature, as are our cognitive abilities and our potential reach—however supportive or harmful. We are who we are and what we are because of Nature.

However, most folx I hear talking about Nature as a feature or ally in their grounding aren't engaging that being from a place of reciprocity or family. They are strictly taking from those beings and haven't even asked them if they *want* to play that role. They haven't given back. Again, a one-sided relationship eventually burns out.

With that, I don't see ecosystem kin playing an overt role in how human persons consciously hold their space, but they do play an obligatory one. They do as they are able, and they *will*, though *expecting* them to do so *without giving something in return* is problematic. From my vantage point, Nature works as a huge collective for the evolution of everything, including human persons. Nature supports everything that makes up the whole in the same way; humans are not singled out or special. In fact, we're the ones who aren't supporting the whole, which isn't to say we can't have a reciprocal relationship with Nature. More on that in a bit.

How do we compensate for the fact that we tire of holding space for ourselves, that we lack community agreement around holding space for us all, that Spirit Helpers aren't supposed to navigate the business of humans, and that Naturekin provide part but not all of our grounding as they are able? What's left to help hold our space fully?

An entirely supportive cosmology, for starters. For the longest time, the word *cosmology* didn't come up in modern spiritual communities.

Now when it does, it's used to describe how we come into relationship with the way the pluriverse works.[2] It can include creation stories, sacred beings, science, religious beliefs, personal experience, and lore. From an animistic perspective, our cosmology holds not just the beings we engage for how we move among but also all of the spaces and forces underlying those relationships and how they work.

When we culturally talk about cosmology, it's always in an externalized way, as if it exists outside of us. I teach it to be more like a community we are members of and walk among all the time. That community is made up of other beings, yet is within us as well. When I teach soul and energy tending, I ask students to explore their external relationships with place, elements, directions, Spirit and Nature Allies, and Ancestors, as well as the internal ones. In the same way our physical body is made of the elements and thus directly *connects us to* Nature, our inner aspects of Self make up our primal consciousness, which is shaped by our *engagement with* Nature. It is only when we have a healthy relationship with our inner cosmology that we can begin to create healthy relationships with the world around us. In order to have a healthy relationship with our inner cosmology, we have to know who's in there. Knowing who we are allows us to better engage the world around us, which makes us better elders.

In my view, our inner, or personal, cosmology includes the mind/body/soul beings within those, and all the aspects of Self that walk with us through this world. These aspects include our chakras (wheels of energy situated along the spine from the base to the crown of the head) or hweols of maegen (Old Norse "wheels of might"), our etheric field and its activation points, our shadow parts (aspects of Self that we don't know, don't want to know, or are afraid of), our Sacred Self (ves), our ego, our personal narrative (the story we tell ourselves as well as the one we present to the world about each of these personal things), our scars that hold us liminally in a place we once were and potentially open us to places we've never been, and possibly the things about us that we can never know. The ways in which we envision ourselves as our own universe made up of multiple processes and perhaps even many selves are all perspectives on inner cosmology that are worth exploring.

Likewise, to say "inner cosmology" does not mean it is isolated or separate from our wider cosmology. Rather, it's a microcosm of that bigger cosmology, held in relationship with land, other-than-human spirits, and the Ancestors.

Again, we're not supposed to hold our space alone. If we explore the innate parts of our inner cosmology that are already in relationship with Nature, we can, through those relationships, repair our animacy. If we didn't feel like we had to do everything by ourselves, alone, if we knew we were energetically supported by design—inside and out—we could have a more peaceful and organic relationship to the concept of elderhood and could actually be prepared for it.

THE THREE RELATIONSHIPS
TO FRITHGARD

As animists, we are continuously in relationship with all that we move among, continuously negotiating boundaries as we move. That fact can't just be understood intellectually or philosophically. We have to know it deeply within who we are and enact it in how we move. That means we have to know *all* of who we are, which includes the parts of us that are inherently wild, the parts deeply within us that never perceived a separation from Nature. Confronting what is between our conscious awareness and those "hidden" parts is where all the trauma lies—historic and personal. We can't become fit elders until we engage these parts of ourselves beyond the projections of settler culture—or at least as much as is possible to do so—and understand how to be feral.

We are Nature. We always have been. When we bring our awareness to that fact, we create direct personal relationship to it. When we become aware of that intimacy, we realize we aren't just family to All

Things, we are also responsible for All Things. Our every action has an impact on All Things.

Because of this interresponsibility, when I work with aspects of the inner cosmology that remember we are Nature, I start with the Old Norse concept of *frith*, meaning community balance, safety, peace, and protection. Frith entailed working together as a community, at the level that each member was able, to ensure that the community was balanced and safe, and every member had peace and protection.

Frithgard was a designated Nature space devoted to tranquility and peaceful resolution of conflict. It may have been a collective ritual space or a common spot for solitude, a sanctuary.

The modern take on frithgard still holds connotations of peace and protection, though it has been watered down to the equivalent of an altar space. It's lost much of what I would imagine made it meaningful, relatable, and resonant. Still, from an animistic standpoint of everything being alive, the concept behind frithgard can factor significantly into personal and collective space. I feel it's a missing piece—if not *the* missing piece—in how we support the natural world and see ourselves as Nature, and as such, it can play a significant role in energetically supporting us to move among life embodied and grounded. As such, it's an important piece in eldering well.

While I regard frithgard as a life force in the context of the Old Norse tradition, it doesn't have to be internalized through that cultural lens. Many cultures have spaces dedicated to peace, balance, and protection, with words in their own languages to describe them. Where possible, exploring ancestral connection to the role such a space played may be helpful in making personal relationship with it. Where ancestral connection to it isn't possible, explore a felt sense of it within and see where that leads. With that potential in mind, I approach frithgard, or the concept behind it, as a good starting place to reconnect with Nature—and with our nature. To really hold it in an interagential way, I work with it on three levels of relationship: the immediate Nature space around us, the inner cosmology, and the entire planet.

THE NATURE SPACE FRITHGARD

I always start the frithgard conversation with the Nature space because most folx I encounter are often more willing to feel their connection to Nature than to other human persons or themselves. I've heard a lot of well-intended animists say, "I like animals better than humans." Okay. I can understand the emotion behind that sentiment, though sitting with it "as is" is part of the break. Where we flail in our relationships with human persons is where we also flail in our relationships with other-than-humans. What this means is that the same places that trigger us with human persons will trigger us with other-than-humans. Where we experience tension with intimacy with humans, we will eventually experience tension when deeper intimacy is demanded from other-than-humans.

That said, when I ask folx to reflect on human relationships in their childhood, most often their traumas source from the human persons of that time. When I ask to whom they felt most connected in childhood, it's rarely to birth family or humans. It's to the tall oak they climbed in their front yard, the neighbor's cat who gave them nose boops, or the ice-cold creek they played in every summer at their grandmother's house. It is that spirit of comfort and automatic relationship to the wild around us that I'd like to take into this next section.

A peaceful Nature space in which we are expected to support balance, be and bring peace, protect and feel protected—as in the Old Norse implementation of frithgard—sounds quite inviting. Actually locating and engaging such a space is even better. I am often asked why we must create physical, tactile representations of our spirit relationships. My answer is that it's because physical representations help us to focus our relationships with our Allies. They create a manifestation point for those relationships and the work that comes out of them and in doing so create a safe boundary for all to work within and from.

Soul tending can't just be about ideas. It can't just exist at the liminal layer of our awareness with no grounding into earth-level being.

We aren't just a soul in form; we are *manifest*, with consciousness that propels us to manifest further. We can intentionally bridge the seen and unseen. That's why, according to Tyson Yunkaporta, "we are the custodians of this reality."[3] We have the most timely agency in the way Nature works here. As such, we have the alchemy to anchor life force into other forms. We can make stuff. But in order for there to be safe engagement between the human and spirit world, life force—and the relationships connecting its various forms—must have allocated space and boundaries. In other words, our Spirit Allies are the idea persons, and we are the implementation persons. We excel at focusing our attention and intention into action—thus, form—and beyond. We have keen agency not to dominate or to *be served* but *to serve*. It's our job.

When we leave our spiritual relationships at merely the liminal level, we undermine our authority to take action in our lives and interfere with the inspiration of our Spirit Allies. And when we make everything a mental process, we aren't doing the manifestation work that is ours, alone, to do. The act of creating physical spaces to honor the unseen of our lives is engaging in reciprocity with them. When we create a physical focus of the manifestation between ourselves and our Allies, the needs of all involved are provided for. This mutual safety is true also of engaging a physical frithgard. In thoughtfully engaging our immediate Naturekin who wish to hold this space with us, we begin that relationship in balance with them, thus are working with them *with their permission* and are protecting them. Frithgard isn't just for our benefit.

Of course, cultivating such a space depends on a few things, among which are the ability to do so, regular access to a personal outdoor space, and the desire to hold regular space in the elements—come what may. While we don't all have the same physical capability to come and go outdoors or to tend outdoor spaces, and we don't all have access to safe, private space outdoors, it's possible to cultivate a strong and supportive frithgard relationship by having a small shrine or altar indoors that hosts bits from immediate natural spaces. These could be living plants or dried ones, rocks or leaves who agree to be brought indoors for this purpose, or photos or drawings of resonant Naturekin. Refresh the shrine seasonally to include plants and outdoor items that are only around certain times of the year or to reflect the different stages of what grows around us. Where mobility is a concern, it is possible to represent an indoor frithgard by sounds and aromas. Represent Allies of the outer frithgard space however it feels intimate and resonant in your body to do so and engage them in whatever ways feel best.

Identifying and cultivating such a space in Nature can be a fabulous ceremonial act to also begin honoring the inner frithgard, the spirit of being held by community in that way, and celebrate a planetary vision of balance, peace, and protection for all.

THE INNER COSMOLOGY FRITHGARD

In the same way that there are other-than-humans in Nature conspiring to support us, we also have inherent organized systems within us doing the same. Consider that the frithgard we cultivate as peaceful space in Nature is connected to an inner frithgard; they are inherently in relationship with each other. If we cultivate awareness of such an inner relationship, the idea of frithgard as balance, peace, and protection becomes even more intimate. It becomes personally felt. It becomes care provided by an aspect of ourselves, which taps into the collective of our immediate outdoor space. Within such relationship we become able to see the reciprocity of the world within us. We literally become community where we stand.

For example, in the way that we recognize fire as a being with agency with whom we are in direct relationship, we also recognize where fire dwells within us, and where we dwell within it. We locate where we are connected with fire, yet we remain distinct from it. Similarly, we can observe a multifaceted direct relationship to frithgard that functions on different levels and meets different needs. As we do when it's a place in our outdoor space, when we find it within us, we engage it personally to connect into much larger resources to meet those needs.

Frithgard can be identified as a role that a facet of the inner cosmology carries out. I think of this inner cosmology frithgard as a function that happens in the background of our earthly awareness, working to maintain internal peace in the face of regular, inherent etheric harm. It doesn't matter what kind of harm. It can be personal, systemic (thus conspiratorial), intergenerational, intentional, passive, or incidental. The sole job of this aspect is to hold our peace. Inner frithgard may be a being in our cosmology that we already work with but hadn't yet internalized that aspect of the relationship. They may be an entirely new being who holds that space, and it may take some time to get to know them. I work with inner frithgard as the consciousness of my nervous system.

I experienced my inner frithgard for a long time before I understood the role they play. For me this being is nonbinary and initially was in constant motion in a large orbit around me. Rarely did they pause their ongoing patrol to talk with me. Rather, we would leave notes for each other in a particular meadow of Midgard (Earth, in Norse mythology).

When I finally identified my inner frithgard as this orbiting being, they were exhausted, not because they weren't up to the task of tending my peace, and thus my boundaries, but because they'd gone forty+ years without direct acknowledgment from me. Our relationship wasn't balanced. As our relationship deepened and healed, my inner frithgard became a personal power spot in my inner landscape, a moonlit grassy patch in a grove of protective trees. They are on the run no more.

Direct relationship and regular attentiveness to the inner frithgard (and all aspects of inner cosmology) matter. While we don't have to tend them for them to hold our peace—inner frithgard just does their job holding peaceful space for us no matter what—we need to demonstrate regular support for this aspect of our care. When we do so, we feed them, giving them roots with which to draw on power bigger than themself. Suggestions for how we can do that are noted later in this chapter.

That said, how we live complicates their job. If we put ourselves in danger, our inner frithgard's ability to maintain balance and peace and protect us is challenged. In my experience, this is an area where taboos come in. Taboos are those odd demands that Spirit Allies place on folx—things like "No cow dairy in my diet," "Make all of your own ritual tools," "Don't judge other persons," and so on. Spirit Allies don't mandate these things because they are control freaks; rather, they do so because our behaviors affect how effectively their influence supports us, and our ability to manifest our unique gift depends on receiving their support. Likewise, when we challenge personal mental or emotional boundaries, we create more work for our frithgard. Our behavior can compromise our frithgard's innate ability to keep us as safe as it otherwise could.

Keep in mind that taboos don't have to be extreme. For example, while my frithgard doesn't outright demand taboos, I've learned that I can choose to watch paranormal thrillers on TV all I want, but doing so flips a paranoia switch in my head that disrupts my embodiment, which complicates my frithgard's job. It complicates my ability to navigate Other, which isn't very functional for soul tending. My behavior doesn't stop my frithgard from doing their job entirely, but it does challenge their ability to do so thoroughly. Sometimes I still watch creepy things, and sometimes I get in emotional jams that poke my neurodivergence in a way that makes my frithgard's job harder.

Companion aspects of the inner frithgard also play a role in this support. For me, another aspect that is vital to frithgard integrity is the Old Norse *fylgja* (plural, *fylgjur*), which means "fetch" (in the "double" or "doppelganger" sense) in English and which plays the role of alarm system. Because the ancient texts only mention fylgja in mythological contexts that elicit academic conflict, we haven't agreed on what it truly is or what it represented to our Old Norse Ancestors. However, because as animists we experience that everything is alive, and we are in relationship with it all, it's worth exploring where this role was relevant in ancient soul tending and where it could be active in us now.

The internet has a lot to say about what the fylgja is, though I most trust author Maria Kvilhaug's take, based on the sagas and Poetic Edda. She translates fylgja as "follower."[4] In a historic context, this being is a primal double that acts as protector and can manifest in different ways. In *The Book of Seidr*, Runic John presents the fylgja as an aspect of us that "acts as our second sense or our animal sense, traveling ahead of us it might return to tell us of hidden danger that we perceive as a hunch or strange feeling."[5] Other descriptions of it are along the lines of a ward, or *vǫrðr*, a defender or caretaker spirit.[6]

In my vernacular, our fylgja is the part of us that is most connected to our animistic awareness. It is part of our unseen—our personal mythology. I would even go so far as to say the fylgja *is* our unbroken connection to animacy and the way most of us experience it is as primal alertness or intuition. It's the split-second realization that something's off. In this way, the fylgja protects and activates our inner frithgard, who is the bouncer. Our frithgard senses the challenge and immediately attempts to regulate the inner cosmology. It responds to distress by soothing us and asserting peace. The choices I make in how I respond to that warning have everything to do with my frithgard's ability to keep me safe. To honor their work in protecting me, I take time each night to thank my frithgard and fylgja, to bless their connection into the dedicated outdoor space I have for us all in my yard.

That said, systemic factors that are out of our control affect our inner cosmology's ability to regulate. If we regularly fear for our physical safety at home or in public spaces, if we are denied resources to preserve our welfare, or if we manage disability, our frithgard is continuously responding to these dynamics that may never have the potential to change. We can only do our best to honor our inner aspects and give them what they need to tend us.

If the inner frithgard is my inherent peace, balance, and protection that is connected to the peace, balance, and protection of an immediate frithgard space around me, why wouldn't there be a frithgard for the whole planet? For all of being? Many cultures have unique templates to inner cosmology. I highly recommend researching what such an inner landscape may have been for the Ancestors and exploring how we might draw from that to become more aware of how we move among now. This inner cosmology is what interfaces directly, with or without our awareness, with other-than-human spirits in our living space, the planet, and what lies beyond it all. The more intimately we know it, the better we can live in support of ourselves. The healthier we are inside, the better we live outside and the more fit to build new, diverse paths into elderhood we become.

THE PLANETARY FRITHGARD

In settler culture, having an intimate relationship with the inner frithgard and extending that into sacred outdoor space in our immediate area and family is an act of rebellious solidarity for tending our basest personal needs and honoring our community. Imagine understanding and cultivating that kind of relationship to a collective frithgard to further solidify that connection and pay it forward for All Things. If we have an inner frithgard, why wouldn't Earth have one? Maybe all of creation? Making this kind of transition from honoring and holding space for Self to doing so for the collective is a key function of eldering well. It may be *the* key function.

To illustrate this possibility I'll share a vision I had. In the half-month of Berkana,[7] March 2020, just before North Carolina went into pandemic lockdown, I saw Billie Eilish perform in Raleigh. It was the last show she performed on her preempted tour. I was concerned about going, though I felt deeply pulled to do so without understanding why. However, late in the performance, as Billie played a piano solo I left my body. I've had visions off and on through my life, and every time they have shocked me. This one was no different.

I found myself in a black-and-white meadow just edging thick forest. An aspect of Billie danced there. After a few seconds she told me to follow her and took off running. I ran after her, and eventually we came to an enormous cliff face. The cliff was higher than any peak I've ever seen and was hundreds, if not thousands, of feet wide, but most remarkable were the many colors, textures, and focuses of artwork carved into it. It looked like a blocked quilt, top to bottom, with each square-ish section a different color and hosting unique drawings and styles of artwork. Most curious was that the figures etched into the colorful blocks were alive and animated, much like the introduction to *The Brady Bunch* TV show. The figures weren't static or playing out a loop over and over. Rather, each square represented a different culture with unique skills and teachings, and their spot on the cliff face marked their embodied commitment to bear them forward. The cliff looked like a prehistoric rendering of every culture that has ever existed.

This vision spanned two of Billie's songs, though it played out in mere seconds of Other. It showed me a slow, calm display of the distilled convergence of every earthly wisdom tradition that has ever been. Every culture's wisdom was compressed into a single representation, holding space on that cliff face for all of humanity, all of the Earth Family.

I cried in the middle of the concert as I sat with the understanding that all of these traditions were woven together in a pivotal pandemic moment to reinforce and reboot Earth through their distinct cultural narrative for the first time ever. The tapestry of their narratives was ancient, though I knew they had chosen that moment to come together as one human-person community to reaffirm and conjoin traditions for the current needs of the planet, to present possibility and caring to humanity, and course correct for the thousands of years that we haven't actively done these things as a collective. It was like a sacred computer software system restore point for all of humanity, delivered by none other than our well Ancestors and Billie.

They were shoring up humanity's long-forgotten planetary frithgard that has existed since the dawn of humanity, and maybe before. They showed us our key resource to tend the broken path. They showed us that we can reengage it and that it is our job to do so. And we have to do it *now*.

I came back to this cliff face many times over the months that followed and began to see it as a wall or ring that surrounds all of life as we know it. During my visits, it identified itself as the Focal Point, a visual representation of a planetary frithgard that has always been and that humanity has intentionally contributed to since it first became aware of itself and thus aware of itself *in direct relationship with Nature,* with All Things. I think of the Focal Point as the spiritual manifestation of what I've heard other folx describe as the ethnosphere,[8] or the pluriverse. I was blown away by the fact that early humans understood that they were fed and tended by this life force and that they intentionally contributed to it so that it could continue to feed their descendants.

During those early pandemic months, I watched each wisdom tradition fortify the Focal Point as a font of spiritual protection for humanity and as a conduit for us to reintegrate with each other and nonhuman spirits. I saw that this ring of protection was intentionally tended from one generation to the next for thousands of years as a cultivated system of support then largely abandoned and left unattended as we grew away from Nature-based kinship. The wisdom traditions came together to heal and bring the planetary frithgard up to speed to a place it can be accessible to us now. It is now prepared in a way that allows all of us to access, sustain, support, and contribute to as we elder.

In the previous chapter, we covered how natural disasters and Christian colonization both contributed to the broken path of intentional animism. When we move into talking about not having to hold our space alone, the conversation around that path becomes more personal. It shifts to confronting how we're breaking the path now—in some ways without realizing that we're doing so. So we've not been able to rely on other human persons to consistently hold space for and with us, we've overrelied on Spirit Allies for tasks that are only for souls in form to do, and we've not lived in reciprocity with nonhuman spirits. Each of these disruptions has contributed to why we don't know about the planetary frithgard. Now that we understand that there is such a force conspiring for our success as souls in form, continuing to operate as if we are alone is not animism, and doing so causes further harm to ourselves and all of life.

When we consider how we, personally, have disrupted our (and possibly others') relationship to that bigger web of support, we start to nudge things we've been taught in our spiritual studies that were misguided, harmful, wrong, or have just outlived their relevance. We realize the ways we've behaved that violate our own spiritual sovereignty and/or that of others, also possibly without realizing. By default then, we also begin prodding the ideas, beliefs, thoughts, and patterns we've internalized as true about ourselves, other humans, and the world around us, some of which also directly interfere with living our animacy.

This brings us back to the idea of planetary fylgja. Ancient sagas refer to a collective fylgja concept, specifically of the horse, referred to as the "fetch of humanity" in English, having been such a creature to human persons. If this is ancient precedent for a planetary fylgja, this means that it is the alarm system warning us (via planetary frithgard) of the harm being caused to the container of our human wisdom traditions, to our relationship to Nature, and to the planet itself. The planetary frithgard is the bouncer deflecting that harm, responding to it by regulating against beings who don't have our best interests in mind, and systems that undermine our attempts for unity. Being able to make that connection now, in a time that we are all sitting with how we're in relationship with harmful systems, is everything. What making that connection means is our relationship to Nature—animism—has always been protected. It is ancient soul evidence that our inherent relationship with All Things through the world fylgja is *unbroken and ever-protected*.

How differently could we have born the disruption of the past four to five thousand years if we had had elders to teach us that fact? Does it mean the broken path didn't happen? No. Does it mean that by just knowing that a big frithgard-fylgja relationship exists, we're good? No. But by cultivating direct personal relationship with both of those inner and planetary aspects of cosmology, we better facilitate stepping into our Sacred Self. We literally have universal, pluriversal support in becoming elders. Embodying our sacredness, walking through our everyday whole isn't supposed to be done in a vacuum—and it turns out, it isn't! We have enormous support to help us do that, bigger than we can conceive.

If you find nothing else of value in this book, take from it the need to realize our interdependence with All Things, which must be lived through our actions and by achieving a sense of belonging to that web of frith that has tended us.

GIVING OUR UNIQUE GIFT

Being able to hold space for those big relationships within ourselves means we're ready to start deeply contributing to the wisdom tradition we hold, as elders. It means we are capable of identifying our personal mythology and cosmology, thus our sacredness, and are ready to live it out loud. When we embody our sacredness, we begin creating lore from it, and that lore lives on. Doing such means we are not just world citizens with responsibility to all of life on the planet but to *whatever version of life lies beyond it and beyond now*. It means we understand that we have to give back to that wider frithgard, and the way that we do so is by living our unique gift. There is no other way to honor it. When we don't bring our calling into being here, we become one of the unquiet dead contributing to the broken path.

How do we discover what our unique gift is? The first line of exploration is to recall what we loved to do when we were four or five years old. For most folx it was running and playing outdoors. It was digging in mud or baking with a family elder. Maybe it's about the mud or Grandma's steamed pudding. Often it is less about the doing and more about the feelings that made that endeavor *worth* doing, feelings that the doing drew through us, that we were open to, allowing our agency to shape us in the moment and enjoying just being in relationship with that flow. I can't say with any certainty beyond my own relationship to calling how other people arrive there, but somewhere in it there has to be those same feelings of thrill, wonder, and connection.

The first human persons knew the challenges of being soul in form and intentionally contributed their wisdom to the planetary frithgard so every one of us would always feel held in those challenges. These were not beings who *tried* to understand the challenges or *had empathy* for the experience but beings who had *survived those challenges themselves, and still kept their empathy.* They had lived experience of what it meant to enter the arena and play the whole game. Moreover, early humans contributed because they knew how human interkinship would unravel if they didn't. In understanding that role of humanity, those human persons, our well Ancestors, created a lore-wide safe space for us to have balance, peace, and protection.

As animists, we see the planetary frithgard-fylgja as life force, companions, a boundary, a complex weaving of everything humanity knows about how to thrive on Earth peacefully, balanced and protected, and how we situate the human-person experience into all of Nature, life, and existence beyond earthly life. We, through our other-than-human kin and well Ancestors, along with all the nurture and resourcefulness of our celestial parents—Earth and Sky—created it, and for thousands of years, we actively tended it. We can learn to do it again.

WHAT WE DO HERE

Despite the broken path and all that caused it, planetary frithgard and fylgja were always there. Just because we weren't intentionally contributing to and blessing them, they didn't stop existing, and the frithgard, itself, wasn't broken. Only our awareness of it was. Along with all the many other sacred rites of our ancestral cultures, the knowledge of this collective cosmology's existence, as well as the fact that we were supposed to be thoughtfully contributing our wisdom traditions to it, ongoing, had become lost to us.

The significance of Nature participating as the elemental container holding all human-person wisdom is important to who we are as creatures of Nature. It means that not only is our movement through life inextricably tied to Nature, but so are our stories and the lore we ascribe to that movement. It means that we are always in direct relationship with Nature and to keep that relationship healthy, we must become and remain aware of it. We must make it personal, intimate. The goal isn't to avoid leaving footprints in our time here but to leave them with care. And while Nature doesn't favor human persons, we are as protected by it as the rest of its family. As the planet's custodians, we must tend Nature well and nurture our relationship with it for those who can't tend it and for our descendants. Nature must be an intentional part of how we create new paths, though humanity must do its part to create them. This cocreating bond is animism, which is family in the biggest, deepest sense.

Where do the planetary frithgard-fylgja fit into the inner cosmology and sacred Nature space devoted to balance, peace, and protection? For starters, both inner cosmology and Nature space are already in relationship with planetary forces and by bringing our awareness to those relationships, we begin to see where we are also in relationship with them. As we learn the parameters of those relationships, we can move through our life in a way that informs our lore, which fosters their growth and ours.

I experience that personal relationship to frithgard and fylgja on all levels as a key missing piece in our personal energetic hygiene, in cultural somatics, and in our interweaving with Nature/All Things. Because of that, before we can really feel into what our relationship with such forces might be, we have to sit with the anger and grief of having been cut off from them intentionally. We have to be able to hold the role our own Ancestors played in that separation and its tending, as well as the role we have played in our present culture to perpetuate it. We can't ignore the connection between our Ancestors' actions and our own. We have to sit with and reconcile not just how those histories of oppressor and/or oppressed set us up for the circumstances of our lives but also how our Ancestors' unresolved emotions around those histories still course through our cells and psyches and the cultural systems that affect us all. They set up the circumstances of other peoples' lives—folx we walk among every day. Likewise, we have to put ourselves in the place emotionally and spiritually to realize, accept, and further our Ancestors' successes. The wisdom of their lives, the insight they gained by learning to elder well through great difficulty while still loving, learning, and engaging their Naturekin, can only come from them, and we must learn how to access it.

Many folx are doing aspects of this big care work. For instance, Resmaa Menakem's work focuses on cultural somatics, as does the work of Tada Hozumi. Each has made strides in identifying and reconciling the intergenerational impact that has affected our personal energetic hygiene, how somatic imbalances are unique to different ethnic groups, how caring for and tending these injuries is complex and necessary, and how that tending must be done at personal levels to address collective imbalances. Personal and cultural somatics are connected. The work of Shamini Jain, Ph.D., in biofields demonstrates how subtle systems overlap within and among us, control our overall health, and can be influenced for environmental health. The teachings of Christina Pratt and Langston Kahn, through the Last Mask Center, offer transformation from harmful patterns through energy hygiene and world and personal Ancestor reconciliation. Bayo Akomolafe's work centers on systemic inclusivity of the wound as teacher, potential, and politicized disruptor. These approaches to interagential relationship are instrumental in not just bringing care into personal lives and the systems of our time but stand to transform new pathways from the brokenness and assert grounded footing for the descendants.

Just as knowing that we are protected by and are part of enormous collective life forces is important to our development as humans, knowing we have a role in tending them is a critical component of eldering well. When we engage these life forces as they are natively within us as also part of our outdoor space and global support, we are honoring those bigger life forces and the part(s) of us that are also big. We are staking our claim in the support of these life forces and committing to tending them in how we live. As well, by cultivating a relationship with these bigger life forces we remove the burdens that we've placed on our allies, our parents, and our communities that are inappropriate for us as adults to bring to those relationships anyway. When we begin seeking support from those larger energies instead of other human persons who are dealing with their version of the messiness of being human, we more fully cultivate our direct relationship to Nature.

As animists, we are more capable of seeing ourselves as fit elders when we draw on the spiritual supports inherently available to us. When we live that support, we are tending the breaks in our own bodies and lives, and we bring that support to others now and in the days to come.

INTROSPECTION

Exploring the Support That's Available to You

Take a minute to sit with the ecstasy of realizing you're not supposed to do it all alone, that there is support out there for you to draw on. Take a big, deep breath, and as you inhale, let it draw into you the feeling of planetary balance, peace, and protection—all just for you—and as is appropriate, reflect on the following:

❋ What feelings come up around that support?
❋ Where do you feel that support in your body?
❋ What part of you already knew of this collective support?
❋ How can you connect with that part of yourself?

Sit with that sense of collective support as long as you like. When you have a felt sense of that support, sit with the grief of feeling that such support has always been there, but you were cut off from it—in part, intentionally.

❉ What feelings come up around that truth?

❉ Where do you feel that lack in your body? What does it feel like?

❉ What memories, emotions, thoughts, or beliefs come up around this grief?

Likewise, as you consider what supports you *could* be readily engaging but aren't, allow whatever feelings arise to come in on the breath and be released on the breath. As you practice exploring these feelings, consider the following:

❉ What feelings come up when you think of yourself as Nature?

❉ What feelings come up when you sit with the systems that were created to make you feel separate from Nature?

❉ What is the actual role you play in supporting yourself? How do you need that support to change? What in your life needs to change to allow that support?

❉ How do the other humans in your life support you? How do you need that support to be expressed differently?

❉ How do the Spirit Allies in your life support you? How do you need that support to be expressed differently?

❉ How do the Naturekin in your life support you? How do you need that support to be expressed differently?

❉ What feelings come up when you think of Nature as family? As All Things as family?

Take some time to make notes on the feelings that come up and the sensations they evoke in your body. Record memories, emotions, thoughts, or beliefs that come up, as well. We will come back to these notes in chapter 3.

Call on your Dream Team to help you process any uncomfortable emotions or physical distress that comes up in your introspection responses. Understand that this is the work needed at this time and moving through it is lore building. It's not enough to just *know* that there is distress around an area or even to know the source of that distress. *Information is not transformation. Transformation is relationship.* As an elder it is your responsibility to act on that knowledge in a way that brings relief from the distress or imparts skills for tending it, as you are able.

❋

Working with Nature Space Frithgard

To create such a space outdoors, identify a location you are particularly drawn to. Ideally, Nature space frithgard is an outdoor spot that can be easily and frequently accessed. Being outdoors isn't required to identify it. If your mobility is restricted, where possible sit by windows and listen to the different sounds in different parts of the outdoors, notice the different smells and breezes. It could be that one's entire outdoor space is frithgard.

While exploring this connection, talk to it, sing to it. Bring it offerings. Introduce yourself and explain your intentions for engaging the space. Ask if it's open to relationship in this way. You may or may not get a response, and that's okay. No one is obligated. While in that space, observe what lives there, what grows there, and who passes through it, then answer the following:

❋ What other spiritual influences come?
❋ What Nature beings live there?
❋ How does the space shift seasonally?
❋ Are you aware of aspects of inner frithgard among other spirits in that space?

The relationship that evolves from engaging frithgard outdoors can be soothing, as well as supportive to the inner frithgard. It may also host safe space for other members of the household, such that everyone who lives there tends its inhabitants, talks with it, and forms their own relationship with it.

❋

Working with Inner Cosmology Frithgard

Establish a relationship with your inner cosmology by identifying what part of your Self carries out its functions and engage them (if they are agreeable) to learn more about how they do so and how you can facilitate them doing so, better. It may help you contextualize inner frithgard by appealing to the part(s) of you that performs the roles of nervous system regulation and internal systems peacekeeping. Wherever you are most comfortable and safe to do this exploration, bring your awareness to your breath. When that feels comfortable, invite your inner frithgard to engage you. Be open to how that may happen. It could be through sensations in your body, thoughts, voices, or memories. As you become familiar with this part of you, move through the following prompts. After each section of prompts, return your awareness to your breath and find yourself in the present. It's okay if it takes a few sittings to work through each section of prompts.

* ✻ What word or name is appropriate to call your inner cosmology?
* ✻ When framed in personal terms and roles, where do these life forces fit in your personal cosmology?
* ✻ What influence do they have over your everyday life?
* ✻ What might they offer to help you see your Self as a supported elder?

Sit with the truth that you contribute wisdom and security for the benefit of all human and nonhuman persons through the planetary frithgard.

* ✻ How do you value your own wisdom?
* ✻ What feelings come up when you think of your well Ancestors having made an intentional contribution to your well-being? To that of the global collective?
* ✻ What feelings come up when you think of making an intentional contribution to the well-being of the global collective? To your descendants?

❋ Where in your body do you feel resistance to doing so?

❋ Where in your body do you feel support for doing so?

❋ How do you engage other-than-human spirits?

❋ How do you know they want to work with you?

❋ What trauma do they carry from the human ancestral past?

❋ How is that trauma apparent to you?

❋ How do you experience your inner frithgard and fylgja?

❋ How do you honor them in your daily life?

❋ How do your inner frithgard and fylgja respond to systemic stressors that have no foreseeable resolution?

❋ When you think of the planet's cosmology and your place in it, where do you feel it in your body?

As relationship develops with these nuances of inner frithgard, carry that through the reading of this book. Where needed, engage your Dream Team for help in processing what comes of this work.

✦

Working with the Planetary Frithgard

Take some time to explore what it means for there to be a deeper current running beneath everything you know that truly exists to conspire for your success, support, and satisfaction of a life well-lived.

In a safe, quiet place, bring your awareness to your breath. When that feels comfortable, invite your inner frithgard to engage with you. Tell it that your intention is to meet the planetary frithgard and ask it to lead you to the place you can best access the bigger frithgard. Be open to how that may happen. It may come in body sensations, thoughts, voices, visions, or memories. Take in what your inner frithgard needs you to about this planetary counterpart. Greet it and introduce yourself, if you feel led to do so. When you are ready, return your awareness to your breathing and to your present.

After greeting the planetary frithgard, move through the following prompts:

❀ What disrupts your ability to believe in a planetary (or bigger) frithgard? What supports it?

❀ How do you feel relationship to planetary frithgard?

❀ How do you recognize your calling?

❀ What impact did engaging planetary frithgard have on your relationship to your calling?

❀ What actions do you take on a daily basis to deepen how to bear your calling? Do those actions need to now change?

❀ What regular practices keep you fit to stay connected to planetary frithgard?

✦

Working with Fylgja

As you feel led, repeat these prompts with the focus on fylgja and kinfylgja. Kinfylgja functions the same way personal fylgja does but instead of dying with the individual, it is passed on to the family elder. In this way the wisdom of generations of protection is inherited. Keep in mind that the personal and collective manifestations of fylgjur tend our primal alertness or intuition. They are perhaps moderators between our instinct and intuition, which affect frithgard. Explore how they are in relationship with aspects of frithgard, and how each needs unique tending to remain fit.

3

Allowing the Emergence
of Sacred Self

Processing Shadow and Allowing the
Rite of Heartbreak

Creator doesn't make junk. Creator only makes blessings.
JERRY TELLO, *RECOVERING YOUR SACREDNESS*

If we want to build compassionate, supportive relationships with the world, we have to first build them within ourselves. We have to find and feel our sacredness, which starts at birth, and before. Many origin stories describe life before life. Their narrative of becoming soul in form elaborates on how precious quickening is, how coveted coming here is—so much so that souls clamor for the opportunity. They wait their turn, knowing that being in form comes with conflict, even hardship.

As someone who, as a child, wasn't very happy about being here, those stories of souls desiring to come to Earth were hard to hear because they have become conflated with the Sethian "you create your own reality" narrative. The implication that if our lives are hard, it's because we chose hardship completely overlooks the many variables of being that are beyond our control and that everything is in relationship, whether we're aware of that fact or we aren't. If we accept the idea that we create our own reality as complete, we also reject the notion that we can be sacred and still under duress, which continues to separate us from ourselves, other human persons, and other-than-human persons.

Why are stories of souls ecstatic to come into form relevant to the broken path? Or maybe more on point: why do souls want to come here so badly if they know it will be challenging? I can't say with discrete certainty, but it stands to reason that based on our understanding of animism that says that everything is in relationship and that relationship must be managed responsibly, being in form must imbue relationship with something that being without form doesn't, and that something, I experience, is exquisite agency.

Being the custodians of this realm means we are meant to value and tend Nature, not for our personal benefit, but for the benefit and balance of All Things. It also means, as we noted in chapter 2, that according to the way interconnected systems of science work here, humans have the most agency. We are inspired matter that can evoke change and manifest more inspired matter. While we are in relationship with everything and everything has agency, not everything is equipped to do as much with it. Mountains have agency, and they evoke a great deal of change—over thousands of years. According to the United Nations 2019 data on the global human life expectancy, we live an average 72.6 years.[1] We have the most agency and a fairly short period of time to use it to leave things better than we found them and specifically to bring our unique gift to bear. Maybe the combination of that agency and urgency are why we are the custodians of the planet. Again, not because humans are better than all other persons but because we are better suited *to serve* all person forms while we're here.

That's pretty special, and something worth waiting in line for.

But why is life in form so hard? I think the answer to that is part mystery and part tragedy. The mystery part is that consciousness is unlimited. It is unfettered by time, form, or space. But when we become form, we embody a more restrained version of consciousness. Form is continuously negotiating relationship to time and space, and I imagine that would be a pretty rude speed bump to get used to, after seemingly having had no limits. That is enough of a fall—or drop—to warrant special guardianship upon arrival and is an ideal place for strong elders to make a huge difference.

While we are all born, we are not born initiated into what it means to hold that role of abundant agency. But we could learn what it means if from birth we had elders who understood that speed bump emotionally and creatively because they had to reconcile it for themselves with the help of their unbroken lineage of elders, who could understand what it would mean additionally to be born into marginalizing circumstances that make that fall even harder, who could help us remember the deep longing of our sacredness to come into form in a way that fosters what we do here, who could help impart the skills to navigate that adversity, prepare us for how to deal with not being accepted as sacred by other humans, help us cope with how this challenges us to bear our specific calling, and hold space for us to rise to the challenge to do exactly that despite all odds.

But of course we don't have such elders on the broken path, and we live among systems that not only don't want us to realize our sacredness but are designed to keep us from knowing it and to disrupt our awareness of our impeccable agency. *That's* the challenge to humaning that isn't a mystery, that we likely didn't sign up for and perhaps didn't factor into our plans or even know would be a problem, as eager souls queued for form.

To reclaim our sacredness is a vital and controversial undertaking. This is why a formal "age of accountability" exists in many spiritual traditions that allows us to choose to truly be born again, awake, aware, embodied, engaged, committed to grounding, and knowing exactly what we're up against by doing so. However, as we just discussed, we are not born initiated, and most of us aren't born to elders who can shepherd us into initiation in a way that awakens, feeds, and sustains our sacredness, so that reclamation often doesn't happen and as a result, crisis ensues. We have midlife meltdowns because our Sacred Self can no longer be second to the ego. We are required to gain the skills needed to survive formed being and once we have them, we must choose initiation. We must invite our sacredness, make space for it in our lives, and give it permission to lead the way. It cannot lead without invitation and support to do so, which is of course the key to initiation.

MY INVITATION TO SACREDNESS

I had a lot of teachers tell me what Sacred Self is. They called it Big Me, God Me, Transpersonal Self, True Self, Sky Me, High Self, Valkyrie Self, the eighth chakra, and so many other descriptors that were completely foreign to my rural protestant upbringing. That exploration of Sacred Self was partly what led me away from the church. I'd had visions and experiences that my United Methodist background couldn't explain or allow and in some cases forbad. In the system I was taught, I was allowed to have revelatory transformations as long as they keep pointing to God. When they pointed to a radiant part of me that couldn't be held within that cosmology, I knew it was time for a new cosmology. I also had to meet that version of myself.

I began studying all things soul by the time I was twelve, though my formal soul education began in my midtwenties, in the shiny 90s New Age. At that time the concept of the High Self was very vague. It was presented as the pure, godlike part of Self that knew the greater plan of my life—what was coming, what had been, why any of it mattered, and what should come of it all in my short time on Earth. It was the part of me that had all the answers before I even knew the questions, and work was required to access it. What that work was, no one ever said. Sacred Self stayed in direct and ongoing communication with Source. It came wrapped in language like *contracts, vows, upper, good, light, bright, white,* and *permission,* and the summation of its importance was that if we achieved relationship with it, we could manifest anything we wanted.

During that time I met a vibrant aspect of myself who called herself by a name different from mine. She was familiar and yet completely foreign. Through her I did feel eternal, sacred, and so well tended by a life force much larger than myself. However, along with her came new feelings that were equally as deep and powerful—profound loss, grief, awe, shame, wonder, isolation, and reunion. My teachers were pleased with my reconnection to my own divinity, but they didn't know what to do with the complex feelings that came with it. They couldn't address my questions around why that felt connection hadn't been evident the whole time, and I couldn't understand their projection that my awareness of this connection should just resolve those feelings. Merely knowing this part of myself should fix my life. I should just be grateful. This brightness-only concept of Sacred Self was conveyed like a constant exam I wasn't sure I was passing. And if my life was proof of manifestation, I thought either I was totally failing, or I was in the wrong class.

For a long time I thought it was both. Eventually I learned it was the latter.

The default assumption of 1990s New Age spirituality followed that if we weren't manifesting what we wanted, we weren't living out of our High Self. And if we weren't living out of our High Self, the passive dialogue was that we were "bad," "dirty," "lower." In short, any aspect of Self that wasn't "upper" was clearly lower, and if it wasn't higher, it was earthly. Therein lay the real rub: that approach to High Self reinforced the idea that our earthliness was bad, and thus our animacy—the part of us that was Nature and our interrelationship with all of Nature—was bad too. That jargon presented a constant loop of failure. Not only was there no instruction on how to form and maintain the High Self relationship (or other inner cosmology relationships), there was no discussion about how to honor ourselves as being rooted into earthly Nature *while* radiating into what lies beyond it.

In mainstream American settler culture, there was no teaching devoted to what that depth of soul in form could look like on a lived, daily basis. Instead my teachers projected what it didn't look like, which was just a new take on how to demonize body—the part of us that is most evidently Nature—by elevating spirituality over all other aspects of Self and formed being. Soul was better than mind and body. Soul was the key to all healing. Healing was perfection, and the key to healing was a good relationship with the High Self.

The message I took from formal spiritual study in my formative years was that because my soul was tarnished by my body, animism was bad. It was a modern version of original sin that kept breaking the path, and because it infiltrated how I felt about my own body, health, neurodiversity, sexuality, and inability to achieve their idea of perfection, I kept breaking the path too.

I doubt that those teachers *meant* to do damage, yet they did. They didn't explore the ancestral baggage around coming into awareness of Sacred Self. They didn't explore how privilege clouded their interpretation of High Self. They taught what they were taught, and their elders didn't ground High Self teachings in animism any more than they did. I definitely didn't mean to damage myself by trying to make their teachings fit my cosmology, but I did, until I realized that how I experienced my inner cosmology couldn't be held by the New Age attempt at describing it any more than it could be held by my childhood church cosmology. In fact, they were pretty much the same.

The thing that I felt over and over was that I had to honor *all* of myself without hierarchy or judgment, but a holistic approach to embodiment wasn't available at that time. When I suggested not killing my ego, not trying to do away with my shadows, or that my body (and its urges) had its own relationship to divinity, I was met with surprise, fear, and outright rejection from teachers. When I realized I would never be fully seen by them, I stopped taking classes and looking for mentors and dove deeply into meeting my whole inner cosmology.

WHAT IS SACRED SELF?

To understand what Sacred Self is, it may help to know what we have culturally considered sacred. Just as we have to understand why we aren't culturally aware that we are Nature, we also have to confront why we don't intimately know our own sacredness. According to Dictionary.com, the word *sacred* comes from the Latin *sacrāre* meaning "to devote" and from the Middle English *sacren*, meaning "to consecrate."[2] Britannica defines *sacred* as "the power, being, or realm understood by religious persons to be at the core of existence and to have a transformative effect on their lives and destinies."[3] The spiritual teachings that have permeated settler culture—New Age or otherwise—haven't supported a worldview in which what is earthly is sacred. In fact, they often support the exact opposite: what is earthly is our downfall from the sacred. When we don't see the Earth as sacred, it makes it more difficult to respect and much easier to exploit. If we can't see the earthly as sacred, by default we can't see ourselves, other human persons, or nonhuman persons as sacred. Again, violating the land is violating human persons.

There's room for us all to come to terms with what Sacred Self is. This book isn't intended to prescribe what that part of the inner cosmology should be or how we should be in relationship with it. In fact, don't rely on my wording for what to call that part of your Self; use the words that resonate with you. What's imperative is that we realize our sacredness, and where applicable, focus our agency through it. My experience of my own sacredness is that it involves multiple inner aspects, or Sacred Selves. I'm more in direct relationship with one of them than the others, and she is earthly as well as Other. In my cosmology, she presents as a Valkyrie. Another aspect is not earthly at all, is more elusive to engage, and is fully transpersonal. They are all nameless and made up of all colors.

But isn't all of me sacred? Why is there just one part or a few parts that are sacred? All of Self is sacred, yes. Body, mind, soul—the entire inner cosmology is sacred. Coming into awareness of personal sacredness is less about dividing and categorizing parts and more about being in relationship with aspects of Self who are in form, yet are still more actively rooted in Other. Not all aspects of inner cosmology are rooted in Other. If they were, we'd never get anything done. Our heads would be in the clouds all day. For example, ego helps us navigate our agency.

I like the way author and educator Kendra Cherry expresses the role of the ego. She says, "The ego prevents us from acting on our basic urges [but also] works to achieve a balance with our moral and idealistic standards."[4] For example, we have to have ego to practically assess our situation and say, "I have enough" or "I need more." Ego is the alchemy that helps us synergize our soul intent with what our form needs to survive.

Instead of explaining that complexity every time I speak to that way of being, I merely describe it as "Sacred Self." Sacred Self is the part of me that knows the full depth and expansion of my earthly agency and strives to express it all the time with the interagency of All Things at the fore. To that end, I'm also careful not to say "*the* Sacred Self," and say merely "Sacred Self," to emphasize that fluidity and not tether it with language. Sacred Self is the part of me that is not only sacred but is connected to the sacred order. It cannot function any other way. It can't *not* support my unique gift to bear.

In my work, I find Sacred Self to be the part of us that's excited to come into form, and while it knows that being in form is difficult, it has no practical framework for why it's so difficult or how to respond to the difficulty. Our earthly consciousness has to learn a framework to hold the complexity of that difficulty alongside the fullness of our higher awareness. That framework is energy tending, or grounding. Our sacredness knows things our earthly consciousness only feels yet can't fully hold, and it safely retains those secrets for us until we're ready for them. The tension in that slight reservation is the base of our yearning for something we can never fully name.

Because of that omission, we forget our sacredness as we assimilate into form. On some level we all feel and are aware of that loss when we come into form, and perhaps more intimately, we grieve the lack of elders to help us remember our wholeness and teach us how to navigate that difficulty while still manifesting our unique gift here. That we endure sacred forgetting in a culture that doesn't honor us as souls and actively disrupts us from resources that would help us navigate better is an added layer of trauma. Part of our ability to create direct relationship with our sacredness relies on our ability to grieve that original loss of soulhood in the transition into human consciousness, which given the aforementioned cultural lacks, is an incredibly fraught thing to do.

SACRED FORGETTING AND SHADOW

That grief is what I felt in my initial Sacred Self work, along with shadow that couldn't be honored by my early teachers. What I eventually learned about my youthful revelatory transformations that reintroduced me to my divinity is that the inner cosmology is all connected. We can't isolate a part of ourselves and set down roots *only* in that part because it is connected to all of who we are. The relationship we forge with Sacred Self affects the entire cosmology (inner and beyond), and even when we have the best of intentions to become gently reacquainted, what those roots unearth and enliven is out of our control. Likewise, when we don't forge a relationship with our sacredness, the inner cosmology is unsupported, and our relationship to cosmology that stretches beyond us is compromised.

Seeing why the relationship to Self as sacred is amiss in settler culture dissolves only one barrier to becoming reacquainted with our sacredness. Another barrier is being unable to identify the places where we've stifled that sacred relationship ourselves, where the way we *live* is disrupting that relationship. We have to be able to see the ways in which we benefit from settler culture and perpetuate it and then realize that *those same actions* harm our inner cosmologies. Our own internal biases and behaviors can be huge contributing factors to feeling separate from our sacredness. They actively disrupt us from being able to connect with ourselves and what we came here to do. By default, those same habits harm Earth, Nature, other humans, and other-than-human persons.

Acknowledging my sacredness was also made more difficult by a lack of a community that could help me hold my full experience of it and a lack of elders who remembered their excitement about coming to Earth and lived through their disappointment to still show up. Of all the elder wisdom that we've lost on the broken path, that lack of access to the lived experience of surviving the initiation into human person is perhaps the most significant. If we aren't set up well for that speed bump, it will affect all the bumps that follow.

As with the inner frithgard in chapter 2, identifying the ways in which we live that are problematic can also come back to spiritual taboos—personal ones, but also cultural ones. When we give up things like cow dairy to appease spiritual needs, maybe we should also examine the privilege of getting to choose what we ingest or understand that the food on our table is the result of slave labor. Maybe the reason Allies have us craft our own ritual tools is that it puts us closer to our immediate Nature Spirits and makes us confront how our Ancestors and we, ourselves, arrived on that land. While a taboo against judging other people is helpful in general, perhaps it's more important to unravel the internal process that leads up to why we project onto others and learn a different process. Even with taboos, the inside and outside are connected. They are in relationship.

When we begin to understand the impact of how we hold our awareness and move among each day, and sit intimately with why we play out these very personal narratives that cause harm, we are charged with changing them. When we don't actively support our inner cosmologies, the larger world ones we say we uphold can't function properly, and when that happens, we're not able to do what only we can do here. We're not being good custodians. Again, it's all in relationship.

As trauma created our perceived rift from Nature, it is also the key reason we don't know our own sacredness. Collective, personal, complex—all unexpressed trauma compounds into survival tactics that detract from our grounding and embodiment. When those awarenesses and states are missing long enough, we lose our sense of power. When we don't feel empowered, we lose our awareness of our sacredness. If we can't value our sacredness, we can't uphold our calling. That loss of personal power is the most echoed grief from my students and clients. I hear it on a regular basis.

To clarify, *merely honoring the initiating trauma doesn't make the wound go away.* Believing that intellectually knowing the trauma is enough to regain power from it is another fallacy perpetuated by settler culture, even in soul-tending communities. It is only when we express that trauma that we begin to take back control of how we are in relationship with it. We express our agency in that relationship. It's not that the scars of the trauma suddenly go away with expression but rather that with expression we cultivate a wider capacity to cope.

So when we feel a loss of personal power and seek to reenliven it, we are greeted by the components of our inner cosmology that modified so that we could survive. In other words, when we can't access our sacredness, our ego is forced to compensate from its limited vantage point of survival. As a result, we cultivate shadow parts, or scars, in our inner cosmology. Given that, in the way that I perceive and work with shadow, there isn't just one, as has been put forth in Jungian archetypes. Rather, there can be many shadows.

The word *scar* is derived from the Old Norse *skera*, meaning "to cut," and from the Middle French *escare*, meaning "scab."[5] Both meanings of the word are relevant to the impact of shadow in that there is an initial disruption from the norm, a cut, after which Self isn't quite the same when it returns to stasis, as with a scab. It isn't by accident, then, that when we seek out the most sacred, powerful aspects of ourselves that we may also meet uncontainable hurt, bitterness, fear, and anger. Our sacred and our shadow are held together by the scars of our experiences.

Shadow parts are aspects of ourselves that fill in the blanks when we don't have the capability to respond to a situation from our embodied, grounded Self. They are fragmented parts of our inner cosmology that distance us from perceiving our sacredness. The creation of shadows is a normal reaction to pain and can occur at any time, though disruptive ones were most often formed in childhood.

One of the most pervasive examples of loss of personal power that I've seen in clients is one in which parents couldn't validate their children's agency. As children, my clients were too smart for their own good, better at something than the parent, or just housed with a parent who wasn't capable of seeing them, and the parental response was to shame the child, to shame them away from their potential. Whether it was expressed through abuse, neglect, or literal denial of the child's wit, skill, or capability, the child was left unsupported, unable to fully support Self, incapable of processing the position and actions of the parent, and devoid of the emotional literacy to process the situation. The lack of an elder to intervene, teach them how to respond, or give them space to express their feelings generated lasting trauma, which showed up as a shadow part(s), so that they could keep functioning through the trauma.

On the surface this seemed fine because shadow parts ultimately survived and contributed to the world, though their developmental refinement of appropriate skills and emotional capacity to handle similar abuses of power (even from themselves) never evolved into a functional, sustaining way of being. The result was that every time a subsequent dynamic surfaced that challenged their agency—on the job, in a relationship, in self-talk—they reacted out of their child-aged shadow rather than their embodied, grounded, adult Self. What tipped them off to look inside to see that the reaction wasn't based in the present was that the reaction was bigger than the present conflict. The response outweighed the perceived infraction. With shadow parts, we have to know to look within to source whether our reactions match the current dynamic, and if they don't, to live into the skills of responding in a more resonant way.

Our sacredness can't truly be engaged without that introspection. It includes our shadows along with ego, fear, joy, wisdom, trauma, and all the other aspects of Self (and in some cases, witnessing the missing aspects of Self). All the things I couldn't safely feel before meeting my Sacred Self, all the ways I couldn't see myself (flattering and not-so-much), rushed in when I did meet Her. That opened floodgate taught me the most about the interrelationship of All Things.

THE RITE OF HEARTBREAK

Heartbreak is the birth of who we really are, and its process is called grief. *The truth is, the only way to Sacred Self is directly through heartbreak.* Given the demonization of body and of what is earthly, the lack of elders to help us assimilate into form, and the way earthly systems intentionally poke our animacy, settler culture leaves no other doorway into our sacredness but heartbreak. I don't mean the events that initiate heartbreak—natural disaster, the death of a loved one, a breakup, personal or systemic violation, the loss of livelihood, a mental or physical disability, or an unwanted life change. I also don't mean the slow-bleeding causes, like the lack of support from family, culture, or systems or realizing the direct compounded harm caused by family, culture, or systems. The things that happen to us are not heartbreak. They are the *catalysts* to heartbreak.

The transformational moments of heartbreak come when there is no external support to alleviate that anguish. They come when we reach deep down into Self and find no familiar support or leverage. That's the point that we realize heartbreak isn't just the devastation from the thing that happened. It's also a total inability to recover within the known skills, resources, relationships, and territory. It's when we can't hear body's wisdom. It's when our emotional range is pushed beyond what we can hold and express. It's when our spiritual path stops at the tips of our toes. It's when our cosmology fails to contain the medicine, or we don't have the capacity to recognize it. It's understanding that the current version of Self will not recover, and another completely, heretofore unimagined one must replace it.

We've historically called this dire point of no return an initiation, a breakdown, a transpersonal crisis, or a spiritual emergency, and we've required a multidisciplined approach to recover from it. We require that still, and more often than not, we don't get it. Culturally, we haven't even had the support to cultivate the recognition of what is needed or what can hold us after heartbreak. As much as these moments have been held poorly by our collective, they have also been romanticized as experiences we should just bounce back from on our own, forcibly find meaning in, and even stalk as a form of spiritual thrill-seeking.

Once we realize the places where our heart has been broken, we come face-to-face with unexpressed trauma, particularly with how it's stored in our bodies. Sitting with the wounding we carry is only the first part of heartbreak. At the root of it is facing that how we've moved among our relationships with the world—because we've had unexpressed trauma—has caused intentional and unintentional harm to ourselves and others. Heartbreak reveals that we aren't who we thought we were. It reveals the places where we lied to keep ourselves safe, where we preserved our own safety while endangering others, or where we were so wrapped up in our own drama that we couldn't be present for others. It shows how our trauma responses manipulated us to protect those who harmed us. It bares the places where we have ignored systemic harm directed at us and others or facilitated systemic harm against ourselves and others. Trauma we've experienced and not been able to express causes us to get by the best we can, which is neither grounded nor embodied. It's also accepting all of the above as the best we could do with what we had and that harm *still* happened, and holding that heartbreak as the invitation to do better.

If the only way to our Sacred Self is through heartbreak, this means we have to equally believe our mind and body, which are the containers of heartbreak. The mind can be manipulated, by others and ourselves. We have to become responsible for learning where we deceive ourselves. This is one of the hardest parts of eldering well: seeing where we went wrong, likely through no fault of our own, and learning to functionally act against systems (personal and collective) that support our bad behavior, our privilege. We can't gain the skills to do better unless we do something different, and we may have to face hard realities around what's truly under our control to do differently. When we understand where we have created separation from our sacredness and employ the skills to heal that way of moving among, we become responsible for creating a life that supports that inner sacred relationship. When we can support the inner sacred relationship, we can see external relationships as sacred as well.

The same is true of our awareness of body, though it can be even more complicated. We've been groomed not to view body as sacred. It gets sick, it gets off, it gets smelly—none of which do we associate with lightness or spirituality or the potential to gain them. Yet those and all the experiences of body are our direct elemental connection to Nature. It is through body that we are family with Nature in life and death, and we must identify and reconcile that what disrupts this direct relationship shows up as illness. Illness is body's language for trauma. Body doesn't lie—ever. Where we can dissociate mentally and emotionally, where we can avoid and choose not to feel, body lives it front and center. Form has no choice but to feel, and that is the real kicker in tending body.

Body is the part of us that has never forgotten our sacredness. It has never forgotten that we are Naturekin. In fact, it has never forgotten *anything*. Body is the part of us that most knows how settler culture has divided us, othered us, and created a hierarchy based on the division. When we feel sacred, we stop seeing ourselves as individuals in a hierarchy, which means that supremacist systems like capitalism no longer regulate our sense of Self or our access to pleasure. Body automatically recognizes relationship where we stand. Form is the ecological depth from which we've always known joy and sentience.

Every experience of our lives (and those of our Ancestors) resides in our cells. In fact, every cell in our body has its own relationship to sacred order. It has its own agency and calling. We are in relationship with every cell, every organ, and every scar, despite not being consciously aware of that relationship. But it may be more accurate to say that they are in relationship with us, and they command how we move among. If there's unacknowledged trauma in that web of relationships (there is), we unknowingly bring that trauma into how we treat ourselves and others, how we relate to emotion, compassion, and change, how we behave in community, how we vote. For this reason, when we even brush against our sacredness, we unlock the unrealized trauma of our body, which holds all our own unexpressed trauma along with that of our families, the land, and every unquiet Ancestor that ever lived. When we touch sacred, we touch scar.

Much like the way we create shadows to cope with trauma, humans are also skilled at ignoring the language of our body, which shows up as fatigue, pain, or discomfort. As it is emotionally, so it is also physically: if we can't feel it, we can't tend it. When we tend the sacredness of our body, we learn the flavor of it, the nuances, the ways it touches our lives, and with skill, we can change the way that we're in relationship with it over and over, as needed.

When we couple the discomfort of sitting with our sacredness at a personal level with the way our culture pushes to prevent us from knowing our sacred, it's easy to see how and why we would want to avoid it. We can't erase our trauma or the marks it leaves by honoring our sacredness any more than we can kill off our shadows or other parts of our cosmology. Our distress doesn't suddenly go away, any more than our pain or fatigue does.

As someone with multiple dynamic disabilities, that's not an easy observation to sit with. I've known almost all of my life that the sexual trauma I experienced in childhood showed up in my body as chronic illness. My body language spells PTSD, EDS, POTS, MTHFR, EBV, FMS, and PCOS.* Given body's front-line stance, we can't apply the same logic to form that we can to the mind. We can't just gain skills or learn mindfulness. We can only observe, allow, feel, and embody, all of which take courage, skill, oversight, and medicine.

---

*EDS—Ehlers-Danlos Syndrome
POTS—Postural Orthostatic Tachycardia Syndrom
MTHFR—Methylenetetrahydrofolatereductase
EBV—Epstein-Barr Virus
FMS—Fibromyalgia Syndrome
PCOS—Polycystic Ovarian Syndrome

The heart is the meeting point of all of this—of mind and body. It is the holder of our sacredness, the tender of our brokenness. It is the center of our inner cosmology. If we believe our heart, then we become responsible for learning what it needs to reconcile what disrupts its direct relationship to the sacred and fulfilling that reconciliation. There is no easy or quick way to that reconciliation, and it requires Dream Team intervention to support and shift. If we accept that the only way to our Sacred Self is through heartbreak, we accept that heartbreak is the only way to access our truest expressions of agency.

WHY BOTHER TO ENGAGE SACREDNESS?

In all, it would seem that the risk of dredging up trauma is a pretty good reason not to engage our sacredness. I can't argue with that, and I won't. What I can offer is that shadow parts have trickster qualities that hold us closest to the edge of who we are and demand that we stretch further, while providing us the savvy to do so. Exploring the possibilities at that edge is honoring unexpressed trauma.

When we begin to appreciate our own sacredness, we begin to rewild. We experience that we are Nature. We are not the system, the system isn't us, and the system in no way serves us. We are connected to that inexplicable thing that we have yearned for: sacred order. In remembering that elegant organization, we remember how our calling situated within it. We realize that all the studying and healing of all the things can't root without a strong practice of honoring our sacredness. We become able to embody and ground and in doing so ask for what we need from our Naturekin and give back to them what they need from us. We become able to value what we offer as elders and begin to understand how we situate between the wisdom of the Ancestors and the needs of the descendants. With our sacredness as our base directive, we become able to draw on all of our resources and make use of *all* of our agency. We move among with the understanding that living through our sacred awareness of Self is living in alignment with that sacred order. It is manifesting that sacred order in form so that we can navigate with integrity and no longer be unconsciously ruled by our trauma.

As we come into closer relationship with our sacredness, we begin to see how we move in the world that either upholds or denies our agency and that of those around us. Needless to say, once we introduce other human persons into the mix, how we hold our awareness of our sacredness and theirs becomes more complicated. It truly is a skill that must be practiced, and in settler culture we don't have the support of knowing that our community is working to the same end.

INTROSPECTION

Uncovering Your Beliefs and Biases

Often the same harmful biases we hold against Nature and other-than-human persons, we hold against ourselves. And whatever biases we hold against ourselves, we hold against other humans. As you you are able, go through the following introspection and exercises with awareness of how you are in relationship with each before proceeding to the next set of inquiries.

Remember to do these exercises in a safe, quiet place. Begin with awareness of your breath. When that feels comfortable, move through the following prompts. After each section of prompts, return your awareness to your breath and your present.

❋ What habits, thoughts, or beliefs do you hold about yourself that are harmful? Do you hold those same beliefs about your sacredness? Why or why not?

❋ Why might you hold beliefs about yourself that are different from the beliefs about your sacredness? What is the distinction?

❋ Do you hold those same beliefs about Nature? About the spirit world? About other humans?

✱ In what way does behaving, thinking, or believing in harmful ways about yourself harm Nature, other humans, and nonhumans?

✱ When you think of elderhood and sacredness, what relationship do you observe between them?

✱ What daily actions do you undertake that support the system? Which of those actions undermine your own needs? Which undermine the needs of other humans and of your ecosystem?

Exploring Your Inner Cosmology through Sacredness

As we come into relationship with Naturekin through our observations of frithgard and the relationships implicit there, we must also explore our inner cosmology. We've created awareness of it through exploration of the inner frithgard and fylgja. Let's explore that awareness through the lens of our sacredness.

✱ When you sit with the idea of being sacred, what feelings come up? What sensations are stirred in your body?

If those sensations are uncomfortable, discuss them with Dream Team members who can help you source and express them. If you feel relatively comfortable with these explorations of your sacredness, continue.

✱ When you hold your sacredness in your mind, where do you sense it in or near your body?

Take some time with that previous prompt. To give it some context, it could look like stating the intention, "I want to feel my sacredness in my body," and then scanning body, perhaps even exploring just beyond body to find where it lives. Some folx locate it in their transpersonal space above their crown, some below the soles of their feet, and some over one shoulder. I find it doesn't matter so much where you find it as long as you find it. When you locate it, just sit with it and what that feels like.

Based on your experience of the previous questions, bring your awareness to where your sacredness resides in your body. As you become comfortable sensing this aspect of Self, draw it around and through the entire body, even into your etheric field, the energetic boundary that surrounds your physical form and can extend beyond you in inches or feet, depending on your natural state and needs. This may happen very easily and fully, or it make take some time and practice to slowly draw the felt sense of sacredness around and through you. As you do, consider the following:

✳ How does your body feel, wrapped in your sacredness?

✳ What thoughts, feelings, beliefs, or memories come up?

✳ Throughout this work, did you feel your sacredness communicating with you? If so, draw that engagement into sitting with your sacredness. What does it say? How does it say it? What do you need it to know? What does it need you to know?

✳ Sit with how this aspect of Self presents itself to you. Introduce yourself using your own terms.

Take time to sit with these questions. Journal about sensing and communicating with Sacred Self and what comes up around that before going further in the reading. As well, bring them into Dream Team work as needed.

Expanding Sacred Self

When you have established a rapport with Sacred Self, and you're ready to take this further, bring your attention to it and focus your breath there. With each exhale, imagine your Sacred Self growing, expanding out until it fills your entire form. Again, notice what sensations and feelings come up and take time to honor those.

As you feel ready, expand Sacred Self beyond body and into the space around you. Allow your Sacred Self to fill your etheric field as much as it can, tracking it above the crown, beneath your feet, and beyond your fingertips.

✳ How does it feel to experience yourself so big?
✳ How does it feel to experience being through your form and more-than-form at the same time?

Again, note what sensations, thoughts, feelings, beliefs, and memories arise through this observation of Self. When you're ready, thank Sacred Self and all of your inner cosmology for this experience together. Bring your awareness back to your general body sensations.

Practicing Sacred Awareness in Everyday Activities

As you cultivate a relationship with your sacredness, extend that practice of awareness into safe everyday activities. My students of ritual often laugh when I tell them to observe the rituals of their everyday as sacred. They have never thought of brushing their teeth as a ritual, let alone a sacred one. Doing so enables them to understand the relationship between themselves and the water, the toothpaste, the countertop, the mirror, and so on. Their perspective of and relationship to those interactions transforms into something they weren't aware of before.

When they stretch their spiritual awareness into things they are already doing, their ability to hold on to that awareness outside of spiritual work becomes easier. And spiritual work is no longer something to be toggled on and off. The same can be true for invoking our sacredness.

Prior to brushing your teeth, cooking, vacuuming, or taking a short walk, call in your sacredness. Allow it space in and through your body and give it permission to lead.

❋ How did your experience of that undertaking change?

❋ What did you perceive differently about it?

❋ In what other places and undertakings could you intentionally incorporate your sacredness?

❋ What other aspects of your inner cosmology do you sense?

4

Prioritizing Embodiment and Grounding

Learning to Embody and Ground Our Sacredness

Everything in Nature is vital to something else's survival.
CLAIRE HORNE, *THIS LITTLE LIGHT OF MINE*

I often hear others discussing our sacredness and embodiment as though they are the same thing, and frankly I can entertain diverse perspectives on that. I know that for myself, the more embodied I become, the bigger my sense of my sacredness becomes. And the bigger my sense of sacredness becomes, the more my embodiment stretches into the space around me, such that I live not separate from the space, and I am no longer solely me. I am a collective. I am systems. Given that, it isn't that awareness of my sacredness is different from being embodied, so much as these different vantage points of Self address different needs through different processes.

This is not how most people talk about embodiment. Embodiment is conceiving as much of ourselves as possible *through body*. It is, in essence, putting body's experience first, before that of mental or emotional processing. For most folx this ordering of experience makes sense. We can accept the value of felt sense without attaching emotion to it, without analyzing it. But can body's experience be put before soul's? Where do their boundaries start and stop? Do they? And when we say "body," what body do we mean? Does it include the place-space relationships we move among? Is body not soul?

With embodiment as with Sacred Self, we don't throw out any part of Self but allow the full range of aspects that can be present at any given time and feel it through our form. Awareness of our sacredness and being embodied are each powerful practices. When combined they are a vital component of eldering well. When we draw our awareness of who we are through body fully and act from that awareness, we begin to move through our day-to-day while consciously applying our agency. Such is a learned way of moving among in broken-path settler culture.

Letting body lead seems pretty easy on the surface. It may well be for some people. That we are in a body seems like a given, though how aware are we of ourselves *in* our body? How aware of our consciousness are we through body *only*? How aware of our sacredness are we when we focus on being in our body?

In spiritual circles we often talk about being self-aware, which could be embodiment but is more likely to be a mental, emotional, or spiritual observation: "I can't focus," "I hear yellow," "I'm happy." Likewise, when we talk about being in our body, it's often purely physical: "My foot hurts," "I didn't sleep enough," "Today I'm alert." Both self-awareness and being in our body describe vantage points of our inner cosmology, though not all of it at once. Embodiment is recognizing through self-awareness from within our body that we are composed of seen and unseen aspects and sitting with the relationship between them. It is moving among with this relationship at the fore. It is holding awareness of our seenness and unseenness at the same time and perhaps living into them as being the same.

Readers with a practice that facilitates being in active relationship with the seen and unseen can engage that embodiment approach for the introspection of this chapter. For those who don't have such a practice, explore what ones are available. They can be more traditional practices involving stillness, physical poses, breathwork, walking or other repetitive movement (particularly outdoors, near a window, or with Nature sounds) or bringing the awareness fully to body. Feel free to experiment as led, even if a solid embodiment practice is in place.

I don't have a single embodiment practice, nor can I offer one. For me embodiment takes different approaches at different times. Sometimes I can accomplish awareness of myself in my body by merely bringing my awareness to where I am, the position I'm in, observing my body temperature and general sensations, allowing my perceptions of the space around me to come in and glide by, or acknowledging my thoughts and letting them move through. Other times I get there by sitting outside and deeply experiencing the sensations of the elements on my skin and observing what thoughts, feelings, beliefs, or memories come up.

However, when those approaches don't work, I use *galdring*, or chanting, to be fully in my body, or I try gentle, rhythmic movement, floating in water, or some sort of physical deprivation, such as darkness or sound cancellation. Other times I find embodiment through talking to each of the aspects of my inner cosmology, expressing gratitude to them, and observing what comes up. And sometimes I have a dissociative experience so profound that it embodies me even more than stillness or intentional being.

Experiment initially with what allows you to observe Self through body, only. Discuss potential approaches to this with your Dream Team. While there are many routes to embodiment, the easiest among them may be to set a timer for three to five minutes and sit quietly, focusing only on the breath. Whatever ambient sounds waft in, frenzied thoughts come up, or physical discomforts distract you, observe them and bring the focus back to your breath. If three minutes is too long, do one minute. The emphasis isn't on duration, but awareness. And as your awareness flickers—and it will—just bring it back. No judgment, no projection, just observe the distraction, honor it, and return the awareness to the breath.

Three minutes doesn't seem like long for a spiritual practice, but it can feel like an eternity depending on your comfort level with observation and stillness. I suggest a short interval to start with, so that it's doable, and then expanding the length of time as it is possible. The outcome of this ritual practice is to teach the awareness to find this state of observance on its own, naturally, so that we begin to move among in this awareness without always having to intend to do so. It becomes natural. Even if it feels impossible at first, keep looking for different ways to practice embodiment. There is no wrong way; it's just a matter of finding what works.

In that feeling-aware state, we move through our lives from a visceral knowing of who we are and how we're moving among. But embodiment is more than spiritual knowing. It's living all of our emotional and physical experience of Self in the present. It is an avenue for holding all of Self as sacred. Embodiment truly is the act of *doing* from the most widely observed awareness of Self, as opposed to just moving through life with no awareness of Self or of *how* we're moving. As animists, embodiment has everything to do with how we're affecting the relationships we're in and among. When we bring our awareness to our body, we have to be where we are. We can't be in another time or place or unintentionally dissociative. Embodiment makes us truly present.

As embodiment becomes more automatic, do daily chores embodied. Take a walk embodied. Cook embodied. Approach trance work embodied. Notice how the experience of Self in space changes. Notice how the engagement of space is different when we truly stand where we are. Moving through life embodied is moving through life as an animist. I've said for years, "Animism is where you stand. It isn't another place, culture, or time." We are already on the path. Look down, look up, and all around. Embodied Self and our relationship with it changes, forever.

Settler culture has taught us to isolate our spiritual practices to specific times and dates: meditation on Tuesdays, guided visualization Friday mornings, coven ritual Saturday night. When we stop toggling embodiment off and on and live it through brushing our teeth and walking the dog, how we see ourselves in the world changes both us and the world. When we can see ourselves differently, we can change how we move among. We see in real time our web of relationship to ecosystem and human community. When we change how we move among, bigger systems of oppression change. We have outcreated them.

However we arrive at embodiment, understand that doing so is a deep rebellion against current systems of oppression that would prefer we stay disconnected, against intergenerational trauma that until felt and expressed is passed on, against forces that keep us from situating ourselves in the ecosystem, Naturekin, and all of humanity, and against the ingrained violence of separation that we've waged against ourselves because we didn't know not to. Indeed, embodiment is a practice that facilitates our awareness, though when implemented into mindfulness and soul-tending rituals, it also becomes a way that we generate change in our lives. In this work we are confronting our responsibility as a relative to All Things, engaging in reciprocity by intentionally taking on that responsibility and rooting our personal way of acting on that responsibility into our calling—our unique gift.

The more we learn about ourselves through embodiment, the more we can tend our unexpressed trauma. The more we tend those hurts, the more we make room for a version of ourselves that—even bearing the marks of those hurts—can be more present in our communities. The more present we are in our communities, the more capable we are in bringing our unique gifts to our communities. We all win.

THE PROBLEM OF EMBODIMENT

Embodiment has become the buzzword of therapists, life coaches, soul healers, somatic practitioners, and Instagram influencers alike, making it difficult to cull rooted approaches from branded trends. Often embodiment is put forward more along the lines of superficial seen self-awareness as I described above, as a gold standard that always feels good or pleasurable, and as a practice that centers Self. In my experience none of these are accurate and don't serve us as elders.

The projection that embodiment always feels good is deeply problematic to me. Coming from a broken path, the practice of spiritual reconnection is going to hurt. It's going to dredge up uncomfortable feelings, maybe even pain—physical, emotional, and mental. It just is. It's not personal, though it feels that way. Feeling discomfort or pain is not a failure or an indication of doing the practice wrong, and it doesn't mean that embodiment isn't a beneficial practice. In fact, discomfort is more likely an indication that embodiment is doing what it can in the moment.

Yucky responses to embodiment bring up personal feels and are an indication of an entire culture that hasn't processed its trauma and doesn't know how to. Settler culture and even many spiritual communities haven't made space for that conversation let alone provided support for when embodiment doesn't feel good. Beyond that, our culture directly impedes our work of trauma processing. This harm and lack is true for everyone in settler culture, though it is particularly evident for folx whose bodies have been historically, politically, and systematically marginalized and still are.

Does that mean embodiment is bad? No. Will it always feel uncomfortable? No. In fact, it may not feel uncomfortable at all at first, or at least not very often. But if our embodiment practice doesn't make room for and have a functional way to accommodate discomfort—particularly long-term discomfort—it isn't much of a practice. A good measure for validity of an embodiment practice—or any energetic or spiritual practice—is this: Does it only leave Self feeling good? Because if it does, I question whether it's doing what it says it's supposed to for our purposes in eldering work, and I most definitely question whether the result is actual embodiment.

The current feel-good version of embodiment also fuses it with manifestation, which is retrofitting it from a state of being fully present through awareness of all of Self in body to using presence to produce what we want. It's a way to codify how we engage ourselves. Instead of allowing the state of embodiment itself to tell us what we need and how to navigate in life, it becomes a way to acquire things, status. For me, this is not embodiment; it is not *wyrd* weaving. In Old Norse culture, *wyrd* is understood to be observation of the factors that influence what we can do with our agency (and by default what we can't do or are not likely to do). These factors include our past deeds, our intergenerational past, systemic limitations or privileges, etc. When we participate actively in those factors, I call it wyrdweaving. When our base realization of the full Self is hijacked in the name of production, we remain disrupted from our calling, sacredness, Spirits of Place, well Ancestors, and elders who could have helped us embody.

When we project always being happy or productive onto embodiment we fail to engage our inner cosmology, which means we aren't honoring our full Selves. When we omit navigating what may come up within us—shadow and all—we lose awareness of the space and relationships around us. What makes embodiment work isn't a state of heightened Me but the realization of interrelationship through Me. We are not flying solo, even in our embodiment—especially in our embodiment.

As I noted in the opening paragraph of this chapter, this experience of interrelatedness isn't how we commonly talk about embodiment. We don't approach it as experiencing our seen and unseen at once. We don't allow intentional space within us for the spiritual and physical. We don't approach body as the bridge to the seen and unseen space around us.

I've been careful throughout this chapter to speak of dissociation when it is an unintentional response, which trauma frameworks describe as nervous system triggers that we learn to regulate. However, we can experience being fully in our body and beyond it *and* still be embodied.

We can be so enrapt through body that our experience of what we are physically expands, such that we are not individual anymore. We can become part of the space around us and still be embodied. We can be wholly focused on our breath and experience the larger web of belonging. We can dissociate ourselves through intentional beingness such that our understanding of being present expands.

Part of what we're up against in tending our relationship to the broken path is that even our concept of well-being and care strategies are colonized, and we can't see that corruption. We are so starved for meaningful engagement with the sacred that we can't distinguish a practice that is not in our best interests or even interjects harm. As a result, we haven't cultivated the lexicon to pinpoint what feels off in our being or with a technique we're exploring, and we don't have elders who can teach us to identify what's not right and how to respond. When we sit with our history of being separated from Nature and how everything from our language to our disruption from our well Ancestors reflects that lack of support for our agency, we realize we also can't take what we're taught at face value. We must question it in the context of our cultural wounds but also within our bodily truth.

Part of being willing to sit with that truth includes feeling things about ourselves that we don't want to feel and acknowledging truths about how we got where we are in life that we don't want to honor. When we endure harm from the way our culture operates, from acts of Nature or even those acts perpetrated against us personally, we cultivate coping skills to maintain some quality of life. As well, where we are more privileged than others, we haven't cultivated certain coping skills to deal with systemic stresses because we never had to. As we discussed with Sacred Self and shadows, the result of these influences is that our inner cosmology modifies based on what we can cope with at any given time. Those modifications work for a while—sometimes decades—but eventually, inevitably, they begin to diminish our power in addition to exacerbating the initiating trauma. In fact, our power continues to diminish until the core trauma is expressed. It shows up as uncontrollable mental dissociation and spiritual fragmentation of our life force, which can include instinct injury, shadow, soul loss, possession, and ancestral trauma. Our first experiences of embodiment, like those of our sacredness, may have their share of heartbreak, too.

Being embodied doesn't mean being in a state of perfection. It means being in a state of acceptance of our all of Self, as is. If our embodiment practice doesn't or can't hold space for uncomfortable and possibly unwanted feelings, beliefs, thoughts, habits, and memories, *we are not truly embodied in those moments, and we will not become so until our practice can hold such.* Just as bringing our awareness to our sacredness sheds light on shadows, so does living embodied. In the words of author Stephen Jenkinson, "We're not built to be happy; we're built to be whole."[1] In short, if embodiment is uncomfortable and/or brings up unwanted things, *it's still embodiment.*

For that reason I attest that our body isn't merely a scorekeeper continuously tracking our trauma, but *the* lorekeeper constantly weaving our story: body keeps the lore. Embodiment isn't *instead* of trauma, but *with* trauma, *among* trauma. Trauma is not separate from us or our relationships. Embodiment isn't having a physiological experience of how my soul in form would have been without trauma. It's not feeling how it could or should be instead.

In my experience, there is no one version of me that I can fully honor or ignore, and that's the most honest approach to embodiment I've found. Being truly present is standing in the middle of a bunch of selves I don't like and wholly honoring that they are also the ones who know more than I do about everything. Embodiment is being able to hold all of it to the extent that is available to me at any given time and still move among in a way that honors me and all kin around me. In the same way, embodiment is yearning for the solace and peace that we all come here with and knowing they are also part of who we are. We are the yearning for peace remembered and the charged reality of being a soul in form.

That said, how it feels to be embodied is different for us all because we are in our bodies differently. Felt sense shows up and means a different thing to each of us. In his book, *Deep Liberation,* Langston Kahn describes felt sense wonderfully as "a knowing beyond words that we carry deep within our bodies."[2] It's seeing or hearing something and having body respond. It's experiencing some dynamic and having information about it come through body. We all have our unique relationship to felt sense, and Langston's book is groundbreaking in identifying, cultivating, and working with it for change.

Felt sense has kept me (mostly) inside the lines most of my life. I have a very clear just-below heart flutter sensation when I'm headed the right way with something. It is this relationship to felt sense that I have experienced the longest.

When I work with the runes, I have to hold them a certain way to be sure that my body is connected with them, and the runes that need to speak tingle in my fingers. In the everyday, I have recognized a variety of subtler sensations through my body that alert me to important details. When someone is speaking to me and their words start to sound distant, I know to be careful with them. If I sense a heaviness in my chest, I know that I need to be super mindful. If I feel denseness in the space between myself and someone else, that is my body telling me to stay back. As well, my relationship with inner frithgard and fylgja are very tied to the communications of my body. Talking with them about felt sense helped me decode some of the more subtle signals.

That said, my relationship with felt sense has been fraught. As someone who was physically violated repeatedly before I could cultivate full relationship with my body's language, I could feel its voice, but I couldn't always understand or allow what it was saying. I recognized many times that my body spoke very clearly, but I acted against its wisdom to make others comfortable or to prioritize my safety. There can be reasons for why we can't hear our body or don't want to, and they are valid and true. It may be appropriate to explore with a Dream Team member the idea that body is a facet of Self that hasn't had the opportunity to speak. Coming up with strategies to facilitate that relationship can make all the difference with embodiment and relationship to place.

PLACE, NONHUMAN SPIRITS, AND GROUNDING

As animists we're aware that we are in direct relationship with the beings around us and beyond, yet we don't tend to think of ourselves as being in an ecosystem or ecosystems. As we discussed in chapter 2, we aren't meant to hold our space alone—internally or externally—and we don't. We have big forces working on our behalf to help us greet the joys and challenges of our lives and expend our agency the best that we can to bear our calling here. The more we delve deeply into our embodiment, the more those relationships take on a more pivotal and intimate role. It can seem pretty intimidating to work with those big energies, which is why we have familiar Naturekin and Spirits of Place ushering us into that collective. Our job is to be aware of the connection between ourselves and our space so that we can assume our inherent responsibility for where we eat, sleep, and do all the things.

Experiencing ourselves as sacred through our body is often the first place that many of us really internalize that we aren't just part of something bigger than ourselves. Rather, we know in the most intimate way possible that we are in relationship with a *pluriversal community* populated with beings both familiar and beyond our comprehension. When we feel that, we realize that while we are but one small part of a vast community, our unique gift is relevant to every member of that community. Ultimately this means it's imperative that we get it done. By taking the time to flesh out with whom we are in closest relationship in that vastness and bringing that awareness to our everyday as much as we can, we work with them with intention, to evoke change in our personal lives and our communities.

Place

Discerning immediate other-than-humans and other-than-human spirits can be as easy as looking around. Whether we're in the city, suburbs, or country, we are situated in complex ecosystems that are deeply aware of us. They are ecosystem kin, the landvaettir, or spirits of the land—grass, trees, plants, animals, insects, rocks, air, structures (even individual rooms)—those you bring inside and those who grow wild. Also, the Jotnar, or forces of Nature, like storms, rivers, gravity, the Land Elders, as well as Ancestors, directions, base elements, spirits of cultures, and communities . . . all of these and more are Spirits of Place. They are unique to location, quite often to season, and possibly to moment.

The connection between awareness of our sacredness, embodiment, and nonhuman spirits has everything to do with our ability to show up well in the world and use our agency to support and further our calling. When we actively begin to cultivate the relationships we live among every day, we not only come more deeply into ourselves and the caretaking of the spirits we live among, we also cultivate the other important component of our ability to elder well: grounding.

In order to thoroughly ground ourselves, we work with place, which implies that we have to understand who is in it. We have to understand that we recognize our space as comprised of beings with their own lore and agency, who choose to help us shape ours. We'll talk more about this in subsequent sections of this chapter.

When we turn the conversation to talking about who occupies our space with us, we're talking about cosmology. Often in modern shamanic conversations of cosmology, it's put forward as a rigid planned-out thing that we absorb from a teacher or the internet, and we're just supposed to retrofit ourselves to it. While mention of nonhuman spirits is made, the emphasis is usually put on Spirit Allies and deities. If that works for you, and the nonhuman spirits are okay with it, have at it. However, for many folx that I encounter in settler culture, the experience of this part of their cosmology is challenging because the cosmology they were given growing up (consciously or unconsciously) doesn't serve them, or the one they've adapted from another source isn't functional.

We often hear it in the context of the medicine wheel, or the circle of life, the roots of which are found in many different cultures, each with different representations. That uniqueness of representation is significant for many reasons; key among them is relationship. The reason a cosmology works is primarily because it is healthy and contains components that meet our needs. It also works because we are in relationship with it—which implies reciprocity. And reciprocity doesn't mean transactional. It's not something for something. We're not just asking for things from cosmology or using it for self-gain. We're tending it, asking what it needs, and giving that to it ongoing.

In chapter 2, we talked about cosmology as the beings we engage when we move among, as well as all the parameters of those relationships and how they work. What this means is that cosmology isn't just a flat representation of the deities, Allies, Ancestors, and whatever other beings we engage. It's a living, evolving, collective of relationships that we must interact with on an ongoing basis, just as we do with our significant human relationships. Our cosmology isn't something we use then put away. We function from it all the time.

Discovering who is in our cosmology is a daunting task for folx without a religiously imposed cosmology. An exercise in my coursework on cosmology is to draw it. Start with Self (comprising its own inner cosmology) as the center of the cosmology. Then draw all the known aspects of the cosmology (inner and beyond) as they situate in relationship to Self. Include honored deities, animals, bugs, elements, directions—everything. This exercise helps folx to give context not only to who or what, and where walks with them but also what roles those beings play.

Also, with more practical awareness of ecosystem kin, spiritual insights are perhaps more vivid. For that reason I highly encourage researching their mundane characteristics. There may be mannerisms specific to a being that aren't easily characterized but could influence communication with them. For instance, it could be useful to know that wild turnip switches gender depending on where it is in its growth stage. Sometimes small details that stump us in deciphering Naturekin communication can be easily resolved with a bit of homework.

When we contextualize our cosmology, we have a better understanding of how we draw on it to shape ritual. Ritual is where all of those relationships become active, and it's also where any weaknesses in those relationships are revealed. For this reason, we should consider that we can only be as intimate with and delve as deeply into our spirit relationships as we are willing to with our humans ones.

Nonhuman Spirits

A fundamental disconnect for me in my formative soul teachings was that they didn't root spiritual practice into where we live. Much of the teachings of 1990s spirituality treated place as where we happened to be as we engaged soul work, the backdrop rather than a participating being. For this reason, many of us cultivated cosmologies that aren't connected to where we live. In fact, modern shamanism still doesn't thread place into spiritual practice as vital presence(s).

In order to really be embodied and aware of our sacredness, we must recognize and acknowledge the nonhuman spirits who support us in those endeavors. We need to see our Spirits of Place reflected in our cosmology and vice versa. A dilemma of the broken path is that we do not have true totems, meaning relationships with Naturekin and Spirits of Place that have been nurtured and handed down over generations and encompass both lineage and region relationship lore. Instead, most of us have cobbled together relationships to Naturekin who have personal or ancestral meaning or who have expressed interest in working with us.

We have to go with what we have, though we need to be respectful in how we accomplish that. However, when we start to focus our eldering on leaving things better than we found them, we have to be willing to go more deeply into who is in our cosmology and what role they play. It isn't enough to just know that a being is there. For this reason I encourage folx to be very engaged with the Spirits of Place where they live. This doesn't mean that beings from far off lands or a past time can't be part of our cosmology, but I do think there's good reason to pause if they're taking up more space in our relationships than those who are in our actual backyard.

When there is disparity between the beings we work with and those we live among, our cosmologies can't support our work here. We have to be able to draw on the relationships with those beings closest to us to make the most of our agency. Even though we're the custodians, even though we have loads of agency, we can't do any of it alone well. So if our cosmology isn't grounded into accessible strong relationships, it can't support how we elder.

There are many other reasons why plug-and-play cosmology isn't sustainable. Foremost among them is cultural appropriation. Few people in settler culture originated on this land. The rest of us are here through circumstances that range from violent and deeply grievous to liberated and joyful. Some came to find a new life. Some came with the intention of subverting existing peoples to elevate ourselves. Some didn't arrive here through choice at all. The fact that the land most of us live on was in close relationship with other humans for thousands of years means that we can't just assume relationship with Spirits of Place. We can't just assume peaceful Naturekin relations, at all. Some indigenous folx have unbroken relationship to ancestral lands and trying to force our way into that relationship is inappropriate. Even land that isn't occupied by indigenous people or that once belonged to a people who no longer exist, remembers. Just because we, through some legal precedent, have right-of-way over a plot of land doesn't imply that those Spirits of Place or the people with whom they have been in relationship will be welcoming, and their boundaries should be respected.

Likewise, I often work with folx who have never asked their Naturekin what they want or need. I've seen folx abuse Spirits of Place, particularly the elements, by bending them to their needs. Generally speaking, Naturekin want to be supportive of humans because they inherently approach this reality from a place of interdependency. They know it is sacred order to tend All Things. So when we ask for something, they get right on it. However, there's only so much they can do without receiving reciprocal support from us, as is the case with our human and Spirit Ally relationships.

Along that line, we can't just assume relationship with our lost ancestral lands. Those lands have been in relationship with other human persons, who may have an unbroken bond with them. And those land spirits have endured other experiences that may have changed how they are in community with human persons now.

While it may be appropriate to acknowledge and even engage the spirits of ancestral lands in our cosmology, we can't just reintroduce them to the spirits of the land where we currently live and assume they will all get along, or even want to. We humans sit at the apex of complicated relationships to place because of the broken path.

I've also worked with folx who flat out don't ask permission. They don't introduce themselves to their Naturekin before engaging them in ritual. They call in elements without ever actually greeting them. They buy a chunk of amethyst from some unsourced origin, plop it down on their altar, and use it for healing work. They don't ask if it wants to work with them. They don't ask if it needs healing. They don't ask what humans or ecosystem kin were harmed to deliver it to them.

Nature relationship isn't all woo-woo. We need to educate ourselves on the lay of our land—literally—and read about what grows and lives there. We must observe what's in our own yard. We need to research the lived experience and science of our landvaettir. When we understand the seasonality of our region, we can know who to call on and who's hibernating.

We can't just drop a cosmology of our own device onto our ecosystem kin and expect those relationships to automatically be cordial, full stop. In fact, when folx report to me that they're not getting favorable engagement with their Naturekin, we revisit how they came to live on their land. I encourage them to introduce themselves to their Naturekin—literally, aloud—and express who they are and why they seek relationship with them. We revisit how to show support for them in their day-to-day and work out actionable offerings that are appropriate for their local wildlife.

Meeting Naturekin more respectfully doesn't mean they are automatically going to be more friendly or responsive. It doesn't guarantee that they'll even be safe. It has taken years of living in my current location for the ecosystem kin to trust any human persons regardless of how they got to this land, and they're still largely standoffish. I don't push it. Demonstrating our commitment to the relationship still matters. As with our Spirit Allies and Ancestors, our ecosystem kin interaction can't just be liminal outreach. We must *do* something. We must give back. Beyond that, it's on them to respond and establish relationship parameters and on us to respect them. Likewise, we have to honor where our Naturekin are in unbroken relationship with indigenous peoples and learn ways to support that relationship. All human persons are custodians of the planet, but some have been actively doing that much longer than others.

One of the Naturekin classes that I teach is solely focused on nonhuman or other-than-human spirits, learning what beings move among us, what role they play on the planet, and how we can be in healthy relationship with them. The class is designed to provoke exploration of what we believe with regard to other-than-human spirits and how we actually live among them in shared ecosystem. The two are often not the same, and that rift plays a significant role in why we can't get in a healthy groove with the nonhumans where we live.

Part of that examination includes researching our ancestral lands and recording the full truth of how we arrived on the land where we currently live, including whose land it was originally, how our Ancestors came to occupy it (if at all), and what cultural or social dynamics were factors in that acquisition. Every recording of this journey that I've ever witnessed encompasses the broken path—every one. In the same way that we can't omit humans from our version of animism, we can't romanticize our relationship to other-than-human spirits within it.

Most of us did not originate on the land that settler culture is built on, and the folx who did were harmed by our arrival. This legacy is part of how we occupy space—even our own bodies—and until we acknowledge it in our spiritual practices and relationships, our capability to elder as animists won't go far.

Grounding

Just as some folx confuse sacred awareness of Self with embodiment, they also interchange the words *embodiment* and *grounding*. They are, however, different things. If embodiment is experiencing as much of Self as possible through body, then grounding is the skill we employ to stay that way. It is literally what we do to hold that deep Self-awareness through everyday, challenging things. Grounding is what moves embodiment from a state that we turn off and on when needed into a rooted way of moving among. To be in a grounded state is to be working the skills that keep us as regulated as we can be emotionally, mentally, and spiritually. In short, it is energy hygiene.

As animists, we ground through cosmology. Through those relationships we gain the support to do our work while doing the work as gratitude for the support. It's all connected. Our Naturekin and Spirits of Place thrive in reciprocity with us, and our rituals and engagement and the way we move among must reflect that.

All told, grounding is the hardest part of this work. Cosmology can be difficult for us to integrate into our lives with so little cultural support, but grounding challenges us at all levels. It's easy to hold awareness of our sacredness felt through our bodies at a designated time and place, in a space curated with soft lighting for our relaxation, where we can focus clearly and not be interrupted. What's harder is to be embodied and work our grounding skills under duress—to do it in real time, in the everyday. Being able to be aware of our sacredness through the experience of form *and* hold onto that while paying the bills, getting food on the table, cultivating and maintaining our relationships, and advocating for systemic change while being harmed by it is a big ask. Yet, it's required.

Grounding is what keeps us on task with what needs attention within ourselves, our relationships, and the world. It demands that we not sink into distraction by scrolling, chasing dopamine bumps, or flat out avoiding what needs our attention. Grounding is what allows us to realize the full scope of loss of the broken path and feel that grief and accountability, yet stay connected to an anchored center aligned with our will to bear our calling. Grounding is our axis for change, and at some point our energy regulation has to become part of how we elder.

As with so many practices of Self and interrelationship, we weren't born into a culture of elders modeling and teaching unbroken cosmological relationship and methods of grounding. We're not taught that our human and nonhuman spirit relationships go everywhere that we go, by design. We're not taught that it's our responsibility to draw on those relationships to tend ourselves. We don't have clear avenues for learning energy tending in a way that threads us into deeper relationship with All Things through our immediate kin.

Grounding is a part of eldering well that is not felt into and realized but is achieved. In order to incorporate it fully, change is required. Systemic rebellion is required. Grounding is not a liminal experience but a continued bridging of all that we are—seen and unseen—through our form. Energy tending is how we give back to All Things for our time here. Being grounded is the result of working a disciplined approach to embodiment that makes use of all the Naturekin relationships around us.

Approaches to energy tending are readily available from many disciplines. Respectfully exploring is a good way to gain exposure to them, though the bottom line is that it has to work, and that may involve venturing across disciplines and methods. For me grounding has come through a number of avenues: practicing dialectical acceptance of my extremes; outdoor altar tending; energy tending, including Qigong, breathwork, and somatic release; sensate focus techniques; deep trauma release along the lines of EMDR (eye movement desensitization and reprocessing); and refocusing pathways with EFT (emotional freedom technique). Although my personal practice of grounding continues to evolve, it includes holding my sacredness in my body while rooting into Earth Parent, then emanating to Sky Parent and experiencing that fullness through my body, honoring any tension that may be there, and working with my Allies, Ancestors, and Dream Team to give it expression.

The best and most thorough resource I've found on grounding is Langston Kahn's *Deep Liberation*. This book describes the purpose of grounding and provides examples of how to do it, all within a context of interdependency, respect, and belonging.

INTROSPECTION

Cultivating Embodiment

As you begin this introspection, take time to cultivate an embodiment practice and learn what place relationships are relevant for you. Be compassionate with yourself and go slowly. It's worth taking all the time you need to come into body the way that works best and to greet those relationships as neutrally as you can. As you cultivate embodiment, sit with the feelings that arise and address them with your Dream Team. Let your curiosity lead you in trying as many different ways as needed to find what works.

Embodiment is a work in progress that will grow with you. Remember to evoke your Sacred Self before you begin this introspection and progress through the exercises embodied. It's important to feel accomplishment with each section below before moving onto the next.

✴ What supportive feelings come up when you are embodied?

✴ What disruptive feelings come up when you are embodied?

✴ How does the practice of embodiment change or affect your awareness of your sacredness?

✴ How does embodiment affect your awareness of your inner cosmology?

✴ How does embodiment affect your awareness of the space around you?

✴ Does the practice of embodiment change how you see yourself? If so, make some notes on that. If not, express how it reinforces how you see yourself.

✦

Discovering Place

When you consider your local ecosystem kin and Spirits of Place, make a full real-time roll call of who's there. An exercise I have done many times and that might work for you is to engage your sacredness and embodiment while sitting outdoors (if possible) and noting what direction you're sitting in. Write and draw your five-sense observations of everything you see, hear, smell, and feel in that space for several minutes, then move to another corner of that space and do the same. Repeat this for each quadrant (or however you want to break it down) for your living space, then go inside.

From a comfy space inside, repeat the entire exercise by allowing your awareness to walk back through it, following the same progression as when you physically did it. Where something stood out to you in the tactile observation, pause to explore who and what you might find there in this spiritual visit. Go through the remaining sections that way. It might help you to know who's sharing living space with you, how involved with you they want to be, and how you can initiate stronger relationship to the beings there. This exercise can be repeated, and should be, to stay current with who's doing what, and how you can help meet their needs. It's also a good seasonal practice to stay in step with who's active when in your region.

Consider your current cosmology.

* How would you describe it?
* Take time to draw it and feel into who is presently active and who may have stepped back.
* How do you honor changes in your cosmology?
* What cosmologies have you been in relationship with that weren't healthy? How did you reimagine your relationship with them?
* How does observing other cosmologies influence your own?
* What beyond-earth beings occupy your cosmology? These could be deities, Spirit Helpers, or greater celestial beings.

❊ What roles do beings in your cosmology carry out? For example, in my cosmology Back (South) is always Fire, and it's where the Janitors live—the worms and fungi who recycle what I let go of. Roles may not be readily evident at first but may reveal themselves over time.

❊ Do you sense dissonance from any Naturekin or Spirits of Place? If so, how you can best respond to that?

❊ Do you find Spirit Helpers from ancestral lands (assuming you don't already live on them)?

❊ How do you reconcile ancestral land spirits with current Spirits of Place or Naturekin?

✦

Experiencing Cosmology and Directions

I struggle somewhat with the traditional assignment of directions, largely because they feel as colonized as our maps and land designations, and I don't resonate with them or find that they have any relationship to the way I experience them. My way of relating to the directions where I live evolved out of embodiment work and actively exploring my Naturekin relationships (similar to the exercise above). Since I live in the region where I was born, I was already in relationship with certain features of the land. Those beings and the directions themselves spoke to me and told me how to orient myself to them for opening space. As such, the directions form the container that holds the space for me to apply my agency. They form the boundary of safety for my work.

While I don't experience the directions in the traditional settler culture way, or even in the words my Ancestors used to describe them, my body has always recognized how it wants to engage them. With that at the fore, I start in the direction of Front, which from where I am, corresponds to North. Having that Front anchor allows me to work the sun's path through the remaining directions. The directions that I work with are as follows:

✳ Above (Sky Parent)

✳ Below (Earth Parent)

✳ Front (corresponds to North)

✳ Behind (corresponds to South)

✳ Left (corresponds to West)

✳ Right (corresponds to East)

✳ Within (inner cosmology)

✳ Beyond (What lies beyond everything I can conceive)

The cardinal directions give us grounding to access the liminal directions. Start with the cardinal directions. Take some time to explore how they show up for you.

✳ How do you sense them in your body?

✳ Are certain ones more resonant for you than others?

✳ What Spirits of Place or Naturekin are in the directions?

✳ What Allies, Ancestors, or other Spirit Helpers are in the directions?

✳ What other qualities do you note about the directions?

✦

Naturekin and Spirits of Place

Naturekin and Spirits of Place can overlap with spirits of elements and even directions. We use these proprietary words to describe them, yet how they show up and how we characterize them can be fluid and overlapping. Bottom line, go with what works and is supported by the non-human spirits themselves.

✳ What Naturekin and Spirits of Place have presented themselves as available to work with you?

✳ What parameters of the relationship were set by them?

✳ What other-than-human spirits have refused to work with you? For what reason? What feelings did this refusal bring up?

❋ On what indigenous community's land do you live?

❋ Is this community a living tradition still on this land? If so, how are you in relationship with this community?

❋ How do you honor that community's relationship with the land in how you occupy it? How do you support that relationship?

❋ If there is no living indigenous community in relationship with the land you occupy, how do you honor the land's Ancestors in your spiritual practice?

❋ How do you engage other-than-human spirits of your Ancestors' lands?

❋ What people currently occupy your ancestral lands?

❋ What feelings come up when you explore how you got where you currently live?

❋ How do nonhuman spirits of ancestral lands fit into your cosmology?

❋ How can/should they be represented in ritual?

❋ What offerings need to be made to the people who now occupy those lands?

❋ How can the spirits of our ancestral lands be in cosmology with the spirits of the lands we live on now? How are the needs of each different?

Accessing Elemental Relationships

Working with elements is about relationship. We can approach them as the base components of form that allow us to apply our agency. Most immediately, they play a role in our ability to center ourselves emotionally and energetically. Elemental relationships can impact how we move among, and we can access them intentionally to affect our embodiment.

To begin your work the elements, start with the basic ones: earth, water, fire, and air. After a while other voices may emerge and require their own seat at the table, including the following:

- ❋ Metal
- ❋ Stone
- ❋ Wood
- ❋ Poison
- ❋ Acid
- ❋ Bone

- ❋ Flesh
- ❋ Plastic
- ❋ Ether
- ❋ Mycelium
- ❋ Plant
- ❋ Timing

Rather than feel like you have to honor everybody all at once, work with one or a handful of elements that speak to you the most. You won't resonate with them all at first, or even any of them all the time, and that's okay. We have a varying capacity in our availability for relationships. I honor quite a few elements, but they don't all seek engagement with me at the same time. When they do, it's in balanced tandem.

- ❋ What elements most resonate with you?
- ❋ How do they correspond with directions or Spirit Helpers?
- ❋ What other qualities do they correspond with?
- ❋ Where do you feel each in your body?
- ❋ What elements evoke sensations/feelings/memories?
- ❋ How do elements affect your embodiment?

Consider that scents, tastes, smells, textures, and sounds that feel good or repulsive are elemental relationships, ways of connecting to the elements immediately around you. How might you engage those relationships to regulate yourself emotionally or energetically? For example, the smell of warm grass soothes me. Tasting cardamom makes me giddy, like in seconds. Likewise, I find mint disruptive; it scatters my thoughts. However, in moments when my mind is clenching an endless loop of cognitive despair, mint stops that spinning in its tracks. How can you show gratitude for those relationships?

When you feel well versed in calling in your sacredness and being embodied, in that state return to the introspections of the introduction and first two chapters and consider how you would respond to them from that vantage point.

5

Engaging Rituals for Caring and Accountability

Tracing and Reconciling Our Life Patterns

The times are urgent; let us slow down.

BAYO AKOMOLAFE, PH.D., *GREEN DREAMER*

Throughout the COVID epidemic and settler culture collapse, I often heard in pagan circles the phrase "magick flourishes in difficulty," which I think is another way of saying that banework (cursing, hexing) is the wyrdweaving of the unheard. It's true that often folx have to take dire actions to set and maintain their boundaries in settler culture, and sometimes that's in the form of magick. The problem I have with that perspective is that magick is more than the language of desperation. It's not supposed to be this thing saved for duress, when nothing else works or is available. Wyrdweaving is what we do as we move among the relationships of our lives with compassionate application of our agency at the fore. Ideally, it is conscientious animism.

The parts of our wyrd that are under our control, we weave all the time, either consciously or unconsciously. We're always in relationship. And even when we're aware of that fact, we either weave at an informed level or an uninformed level, and with bias. The more informed we are about the impact of how we move among, the more embodied and grounded we are, the healthier we are, and the healthier the relationships we influence become. The more stable we are, the more stable our communities are and the better we can engage the Ancestors and be conscientious in how we elder.

The word *ritual* comes from the Latin *ritualis*, meaning "that which pertains to rite (*ritus*)," meaning a "way" or "custom." We commonly approach rituals as a set of sacred actions performed for safe passage into the unseen and rooting some aspect of the unseen into the everyday. These actions could mark rites of passage, family or community traditions, or magickal rituals, such as consecration or divination.

As I noted in the introduction to this book, I don't prescribe components of cosmology or ways in which one should personally engage with them. It is not possible for me to do so with integrity. I take the same approach to ritual in this chapter in that I merely *describe* the rituals we most lack in how we elder now and the components that are significant in them; if and how you use them is up to you.

Is it possible to implement the rituals given by me, another teacher, or some other resource? Absolutely. If cultural permission has been given to do so and those rituals meet your needs, by all means proceed. Is it okay to do a ritual the exact same way over and over? Sure. Again, if it meets the need, that's fine. And if you tweak a ritual based on need, that's fine as well. Regardless of your approach, I encourage you to explore your own sacredness, embodiment, and relationship to human and other-than-human spirits around you to learn how those beings need to be included in ritual and to learn community in that sense.

For the purpose of this book, I focus on ritual to intentionally weave our wyrd, so that we stand in a truthful place regarding the broken path, learn to weave our sacred intentions through our actions in the day-to-day to heal ourselves, our unquiet dead, our communities, and descendants, to hear the wisdom of our Ancestors, and to leave a blueprint of rituals for our descendants to adapt to the needs of their time. So many rituals are needed, though the ones I feel most pressed to describe are ones that center on caring and accountability at personal and collective levels. These rituals encompass grief tending, protection and banishment, shadow tending, dying well and reconciliation, death-walking the unquiet dead, and Ancestor tending. Each of these speaks in their own way to being accountable to our feelings and experiences, and how the way in which we deal with them (or don't) shapes how we move among.

It would take a book on each of these approaches to ritual to do justice to the balance they can bring to our life and work. My hope is that in presenting a basic understanding of ritual and the value that ritual components can bring to eldering well, it will inspire you to find new ways of engaging cosmology and your Dream Team and to learn more about how ritual can deeply affect how we use our agency. One thing I ask in presenting these ritual approaches is to do something different with them. Approach them in a way that is out of the norm and challenges the synapses. When we engage ritual it's not to create an outcome but to invite possibility. To do that with cunning and heart, we have to be willing to do something different. We have to challenge ourselves and our relationships.

In the early chapters of this book, we talked about how the loss of access to ancient sacred lands also meant a loss of traditional rituals. That threading of Naturekin into the human persons' day-to-day not only kept humanity in close awareness of the health of their region and gave them instruction on how to tend it, it also kept them in a place of reciprocity with those Naturekin. Their own health and well-being was reflected in those relationships. Despite the broken path, through ritual we can still honor ourselves and our calling, as well as our human community and nonhuman community. We can work with ritual as a way to express our relationship to the unseen and the elegant organization of All Things.

We don't have a long history of sustaining rituals in settler culture either because we haven't been allowed to practice rituals that suit our spiritual needs, we associate rituals with the church and thus choose renegade spirituality that isn't rooted in place instead, the rituals we've used didn't truly meet our needs, or we haven't learned how to intentionally thread the mundane tasks of life into their sacredness. The bottom line is we don't value ritual in our everyday lives as a strong spiritual practice that roots us in Self, community, Naturekin, and place.

That lack of supportive ritual is part of the broken path. Ritual is what knowingly stitches the human experience back into its inherent relationship with Nature. It affirms who we are and what we do here and acknowledges our Nature kinship.

Nature *is* ritual. It is the felt experience and wisdom of seasonality, of sacred order, which we engage and also affect in our time here. Our ability to tap into and engage that greater story that's playing out is the basis of all wyrdweaving. It is using our agency with intention. It either passes us by, and we stay locked in our own stories of trauma, hardship, even privilege—all of which are very real and lived—or we come to understand that those life experiences are personal expressions of our relationship to that seasonality. They are where our experience of the seasonality has been recreated. They are not *the* seasonality. They are not the narrative, itself. It is our job to intentionally access the greater seasonal narrative and do our part within it. Of course as we've previously covered, active components of settler culture prevent us from carrying out that job and from learning how to do it.

That greater seasonal narrative holds cycles at work here that are bigger than us, bigger than our desires, dreams, or even traumas, and Nature is a key part of that bigger organization. Our Ancestors knew about these timeless cycles in which Nature moves and flexes, and they knew how to move with them by interpreting the messages of their Naturekin and Spirits of Place. They also understood that when humanity doesn't move with these cycles, all involved suffer—humanity, Naturekin, and nonhuman spirits.

Historically, if we didn't honor these great cycles, there were very practical repercussions, such as going hungry all winter or getting sick.

We suffered in ways that left us unable to leave the planet better than we found it. For this reason, our Ancestors put things in place to prevent that separation from happening. Their rituals rooted into the Spirits of Place and honored and contributed to frith, all permutations of frithgard, Nature, each other, and their communities, Ancestors, and descendants.

There are very real, lived global effects of humanity's failure to move in relationship with that greater narrative now, including climate change and the ensuing migration away from affected areas, the destruction of forests, the stripping of land for redundant fuel sources, night sky and air pollution, the removal of indigenous caretakers from their ancestral lands, dissonance from natural medicine, and so on. These current conditions are the result of breaking ancestral traditional rituals that were specifically designed to keep violent outcomes from happening.

All of this, and we haven't even begun to touch on the spiritual ramifications of these problems. When we become cut off from that greater elegant organization, All Things are harmed. Balance beyond our scope to grok is disrupted. When we aren't in touch with natural rhythms in that intimate seasonal soul way, we aren't supported as we need to be for the work we came here to do. We aren't able to support our communities. We become absorbed in the drama of being human at personal and collective levels and may not even know that a wider story is playing out. We forget how we as humans are supposed to work with the unseen and become overreliant on Allies. We don't get to bear our unique gift, and that lack causes harm that ripples out.

However, when we can come back to the human-person responsibilities in form, when we can feel them in our bones and realize that our traumas aren't our calling, we learn to hold the attributes of our lives and position ourselves so that we are still moving among with the greater seasonality. They key to this coming back is having rituals that work for us. We can't elder well without them.

CREATING A SUSTAINING RELATIONSHIP TO RITUAL

To engage in ritual in sacred space is to bridge the seen and unseen worlds for some purpose. That purpose could be to invite something or to honor something, which is often considered ceremony. In order to create an appropriate ritual, we have to understand the intention for doing so. When I teach beginners to create ritual, I start with a very basic recipe: embodiment + place = sacred space.

Embodiment combined with place yields the space for ritual. "Sacred space" is another way of saying "with intention." The relationship between grounding and ritual is vital. It is in relationship with place that we fully embody and ground into our agency, so that we can engage ritual well. Our rituals perform best when we truly are where we stand—when we are embodied, when we are in lived awareness of our relationship to Naturekin. The more we bring our sacredness through our body and engagement with the world around us, the stronger our relationship with everything becomes. As we are in relationship with the place-space and the beings who dwell in it (those in form and those not), they affect our embodiment. As we discussed in chapter 2, we don't hold our space alone.

With ritual, we aren't just placing fond trinkets about and crafting just the right words by candlelight to meet a need. With the community of our place we're creating a unique moment in space-time in which we carry out some sacred engagement. The best way to greet that space is by knowing who we are as much as possible, knowing who that space is, and who we're asking to meet us in it, so that we understand who's doing what within it. In other words, we need to know our cosmologies intimately, and we accomplish that by being in strong relationship with our nonhuman spirits.

For that reason, before I teach ritual I encourage students to be very clear in their place-space relationships. Often when I say that, thoughts immediately go to Spirit Allies. However, how we describe our spirit relationships is very personal, and in my experience to have a healthy relationship to place-space means to actively be aware of and engage the beings who share living space with me. And while my Spirit Allies are very important, they anchor beyond Earth and thus don't share my living space. However, the other-than-human spirits of Nature, the landvaettir, very much do share my space and are vocal and engaged about that fact.

EMBODIMENT, PLACE, SPACE: NOW WHAT?

When we stand embodied at the center of our cosmology, we're fit to use our agency. We're ready to meet what thoughtful, compassionate application of our agency brings. Ritual is a place in which we can merge that human capability to manifest in form with the support of our Naturekin, Allies, and Ancestors to generate change. The way we do that is by using ritual to engage our cosmology.

We've talked about the fact that what we want to see in our lives and in the world can't just be liminal. However sacred our visions are, they can't just be left to a mental or esoteric exercise with an expectation of change. We have to take action in our lives to root the wisdom, prayers, requests, and offerings we're given into formed being. We have to bring them into our lives and honor their agency to go forward as they will.

This is why there is so much emphasis on altars, shrines, and fetishes in soul tending. Through these physical manifestations we recognize all of the Spirit Helpers who walk with us and express gratitude toward them. We evoke our sacredness and our cosmology to each do their own part in what's needed—to enliven their agency on the subject. That evocation of the sacredness of all involved is the key starting point of ritual.

Sacred Space

When we acknowledge the sacredness of all who are in the room (and of the room itself) and formally invite them to participate in our rituals, we are creating sacred space. We are shaping our relationships to hold themselves in a very particular way, for a particular reason. Some folx call this opening space, opening a circle, calling in the space, calling in the directions.

You might ask, "Isn't all space sacred? Weren't the directions, elements, and all the Naturekin already in the room? Why do we need to ask them in?" Yes, all space is sacred, and yes, they were already in the room, but they weren't necessarily paying attention to us. They have their own lives and agency. We formally call them in for the same reason that we ring a doorbell when we go to someone's home: respect and preparation. Even when they're expecting us, we don't just barge in. We at least knock out of courtesy to let them know we're there. We give them a chance to transition themselves away from their current focus and to prepare for the reason of our visit.

Most often when folx express to me that they aren't getting the support they need from their cosmology, it's because they aren't approaching it in this way. They aren't approaching it with reverence. They aren't creating a supportive space for the work to be done; they're just cutting straight to the ritual itself. This is a very common shortcut in settler culture, largely because our production-driven daily lives don't leave room or energy for us to cultivate sacred space—or healthy cosmology, for that matter. It's all we can do to get supper on the table.

Again, the oversight isn't a personal one, it's a cultural one. And even if the creation of sacred space is omitted, the ritual can still produce beneficial results. But it doesn't create a sustainable relationship container for any being involved. No one can work and continue to do their best without supportive conditions. It's the same with spirit relationships. Without creating sacred space for the big work of our lives, we're not honoring the relationships that support that work or creating the best conditions for the impact that work can have.

That said, most of us work best with a transition. We need time and space to change gears, so that we can bring our full focus to our work. We can accomplish that transition in an infinite number of ways, depending on our personality, neurology, culture, mood, lineage, and preferences.

While I encourage curious exploration of how others accomplish creating sacred space, asking your own cosmology is the way to go. We can learn from what other people do, but we have to find the relationship to what actually works for our cosmology and is respectful to the traditions of others. Understanding in which direction Allies, Ancestors, deities, and Naturekin sit and the order of operations for bringing everyone together is an important part of communicating with nonhuman spirits. We need to know who's in the room and what function they serve so that we can clearly communicate our intention for the ritual to them. That gathering may not look the same for every ritual, and how we shape the space depends on what's needed. For instance, I call in space differently for virtual group rituals than I do for rituals I'm engaging in alone or with others in person.

When it comes to opening sacred space, I tell students of soul tending the same thing I tell students of *galdr* (chant)—it should be felt in body. There should be a "shazam" even if it's just a tingle. When I call in my cosmology, I first ask in the Earth and Sky Parents, taking time to heartfully acknowledge each one. For me that acknowledgment has a full-body resonance that lets me know they're present. Sometimes it's also visual—I see their misty forms step forward into the space alongside me. I then ask in directions, ideally facing each as I call them in, then the elements. When I'm not feeling well, I call them in while seated, though imagine myself facing each direction. I also feel body resonance when they enter. I then ask in specific Allies and Ancestors, depending on the need. Finally, I evoke my sacredness. If others are participating in the ritual, I call in their sacredness. If the ritual includes a regular group, I call in the spirit of that group. When the full role has been called, I progress to stating the intention for the ritual.

Intentions

In order to do what we want to do, we have to first know what that is. Being clear in our intention for ritual allows us to know what we're doing, why we're doing it, how to do it in a way that honors all involved, and when the need has been met and to identify what action we need to take to root the information brought back into form. If we're not sure of our reason for a ritual, we can't expect our Allies or Ancestors to know either. If they don't know, they can't contribute their part to it.

Setting intention for ritual can be tricky, though simplicity is always best. My go-to technique is to word it, though it could be set in the form of art or felt sense. I go with words because brief, clear intentions are easy to remember when in altered space, which is why I always advise students to be short and sweet in their wording and to write it down. It can be hard to recall the wording in altered space. Further, confusion can be allayed by crafting intentions as statements rather than questions. Statements allow us to be affirmative and assertive, and that power is what activates the relationship of all involved—including what is needed or desired.

While you can think about how your intention needs to be crafted, the most important point is to *feel* it. Otherwise you can get too caught up in the words and lose the thread of felt sense. Being clear about both is ideal, though if the words just aren't coming, felt sense is plenty.

Crafting Ritual

Because for most of us, ancestral rites and rituals were lost, we have to come back into a way of moving within our Selves—through our sacredness, embodiment, and relationship to place—to locate and live through new ones. Take plenty of time to clarify the intention for ritual and to devise the most meaningful way to open sacred space with it in mind. Practice both for their own sake before even venturing into ritual. The words we speak convey our truth, and it's wondrous to feel the synergy of our intention and space merge. The space we create sets the tone for the relationship to what we're actually doing in the space, to where we enliven our truth. Make it personal. Be fully present to it. Be kin with it. Be playful with it.

Remember to engage personal sacredness and the inner cosmology that wishes to be present. Invite Allies and Ancestors who can best contribute to the ritual and engage energetic hygiene as needed throughout. When that depth of intimacy is felt, begin growing relationship to the rituals explored in the sections below. These rituals of fit elderhood are merely starting places for evolving ritual deeper to meet personal, collective, and familial needs.

Grief Tending

In death doula training, I learned that the difference between mourning and grief is that mourning is external, grief is internal. Where grief is our inner response to loss, mourning is the expression of grief. When we tend our grief, we give it our awareness, attention, trust, fear, and hope. We surrender our beingness to an unknowable experience of becomingness. Grief, in the moment, often feels inexpressible, which makes mourning difficult to do.

Grief may be the most polarizing state of being that we experience. It decenters and displaces us from our usual coping skills. There is no bargaining with grief; it grants no one special favors, and it puts us front and center with the uncontrollable. How we grieve—or don't grieve—is directly related to our ability to acknowledge and express trauma, and historically, we have not been permitted to do either. In fact, how we process loss in settler culture is practically nonexistent. We don't dance our pain or wail our anguish. In settler culture we don't generally allot enough time for grief and are expected to maintain productivity and engagement.

When we don't make space for mourning, we shut down. We become cut off from our relationships—human and nonhuman. We disengage from the wound, even though we are still in relationship with it. We stop expressing our agency. We lose connection to our calling. In this way, unexpressed grief becomes trauma, which comes out in our relationship interactions and is passed on to our descendants. We are accountable for how our grief affects us, those among us, and those who come after us.

I was first introduced to this perspective in the 1990s, in the book, *Feelings Buried Alive Never Die*, by Karol Kuhn Truman. Most of the messaging of that book misses the mark for me now, but the core truth that feelings are alive and must be given expression inspired the understanding that feelings have their own agency, and their livelihood—and ours—depends on us expressing them. They are not built to stay stuck in us any more than we are built to harbor them.

In order to stay true to our own needs, relationships, and lineage, we have to find ways that help us express feelings in a way that doesn't harm anyone yet gets them thoroughly on their way.

Grief can come with many dynamics. We may grieve the loss of a loved one, something very exact and with felt parameters. We can also grieve loss that is less distinct though still very personal, such as loss of a sense of home, ability, purpose, lineage, identity, Self. These are common griefs cited in settler culture from the side of the colonized and the beneficiaries of colonization—even the descendants who benefit from colonization are still displaced from ancestral lands/rites and carry their own trauma of displacement, though they aren't likely to realize it. These griefs are often long-standing and unmourned. We may carry grief for human atrocities, natural disasters, and the distress of the planet. These hurts may be more collective, but we still feel them in our bodies and nervous systems.

Grief is a feeling we culturally have little outlet to express, yet it has a profound impact on how we move among. To tend our grief we must be willing to feel it, which is very likely going to involve Dream Team support. It should involve them, actually. To serve community we also need to be able to turn to community. We need to be willing to cover all our inner cosmology bases of expression, which center body, mind, and soul. Ritual components that support mourning may include:

- Singing to the feelings.
- Singing to the loss.
- Allow loss and feelings to wail through you.
- Singing the feelings into a fetish, such as a stone, pinecone, feather, or bowl of water, then returning that fetish to the land, air, or water for the elements to tend.

- Dancing as mourning, regulation, alone, or in community.
- Recapitulating the full experience of loss with as much detail as possible into an artistic rendering, writing, or song, and upon completion of the rendering, burning it and returning the ashes to the land to be absorbed, or to moving water to be carried away. This ritual often takes several days.
- Facilitating a funeral for the feelings and aspects of Self that are ready to be released.

Protection

In spiritual circles discussion of protection and banishment comes up often. Protection and banishment rituals are done to stay spiritually healthy by warding off harmful spirits or energies. When I began working with my Spirit Allies decades ago, I would ask them what banishment I needed to do, what routine clearing and protective rituals I should do and at what interval. They would reply without hesitation, "Our relationship is the container. Our relationship forms the boundary. We are that protection for you." Their response always underscored that the intimacy we'd created in our cosmology was the protection I needed. I nodded, went on about my life, and made offerings to them regularly.

I'd see witchy friends placing salt and crystals about, engaging various deities or runes for protection. I would check in again with my allies and get the same answer.

After having a depossession with some tricky context, I brought the question up again, and got the same answer, but it didn't feel right. If I needed a depossession, yet I was protected by continuously fostering my ally relationships, how did I pick up that harmful attachment?

When I reach stalemates with Spirit Allies, I reintroduce myself. Apparently that time I provided new details. "I'm Kelley. I've always lived in North Carolina. I'm on a broken path because I have no direct link into ancestral spiritual traditions, and even though I came to an animistic path through my grandfather, I found soul work after personal trauma . . ."

They stopped me short and told me to go banish.

The thing that I hadn't understood even with decades of intentional ally relationship was I thought they knew I had no spiritual elders. They didn't. I thought they saw directly into my life and could discern whatever they needed to know. They couldn't. I thought they knew about the broken path. They didn't, at least not regarding my trajectory. They hastily explained to me that yes, the relationship *is* the container of protection *when it's been cultivated and vetted across generations by principled elders who are fully vested in keeping soul tech safe across time and place, which implies they are still doing that along with me, now.* In other words it would still work that way had I grounded, skilled elders sustaining that ancestral and ecosystem web of protection alongside me. Yet that wasn't the case for me, and is not the case for most folx.

That realization sat heavily for me and my allies, who went on to affirm that long-vetted protection can be revived through my own engagement of banishing rituals in relationship with my cosmology, Ancestors, and allies and by slowly widening those rituals to include my family and living space, my ecosystem. They taught me to weave my truncated protection tradition back to my Ancestors and what was, so that we are all participating in carrying that protection for each other.

And of course protection and banishing aren't as simple as individual energies we pick up. As we've touched on in earlier chapters, we live in a culture that doesn't just not support our health and vitality, it actively works against us being well. We live in a culture that incites continual emotional and transpersonal crisis, and there's only so much we can do for it not to stick to us. In a way, our culture *is* a possessing entity that we—and our spirit allies—have to work for us not to be consumed by. While protection rituals can't stop that, they can fortify us in it.

As well, we can set our spiritual and energetic boundaries with respect to all life. We can be compassionate, yet still be very firm in setting boundaries with what causes us harm.

Banishing rituals can also be very simple. Diné artist and activist, Pat McCabe, Woman Stands Shining, expresses protection in the form of resistance, with the words, "I do not consent to . . ." Her approach to banishing is direct, non-judgmental, yet conveys clear withdrawal of support from the harmful dynamic.[1]

The protection and banishing ritual I use most often resembles prayer and a statement of boundaries along the lines of, "I only allow what strengthens my relationship with All Things, physically, mentally, emotionally." I begin by naming specific aspects of my inner cosmology, then move outward to include my home, my family, my community, etc. Each layer of the focus brings me more deeply into felt sense of the protection working.

Some approaches to helpful protection and banishing include:

- Introduce yourself to your cosmology, *in detail*. Express to it what resources you have and what ones you don't. Express personal vulnerabilities and what needs must be met. Express the collective marginalization you are most impacted by and what's needed to keep you safe in community, in public, in your life. Ask for what you need in detail.

- Explore your relationship to "good and evil." Note how they show up in your cosmology, where you feel each in your body, and how they are embodied in your life. When you have a felt relationship to those energies, use those feelings as the base around which you craft ritual. For example, the heart of my banishment ritual is the wording "strengthens my relationship with All Things," because this state of being is the greatest experience of Oneness for me. Anything that interferes with that, with my sense of belonging, or that attempts to disrupt me from interdependence is not functioning with my needs or well-being in mind. Dialing that sense of impenetrable relationship into every level of myself, every aspect of life that I can conceive of is protection for me.

- Ask an Ancestor who is skilled in human-person protection and banishing to work with you on creating rituals to keep you safe.

- Consider how your energy hygiene practice could bring balance in your body and field, and consult the Dream Team member who can help you reach that balance.

Shadow Tending

In chapter 3, we discussed that Sacred Self and shadow parts are indivisible. They are in relationship with each other via our scars. It is not possible to engage our sacredness without also coming to know our shadow aspects. The inverse is also true: we can't engage our shadow aspects without also greeting our sacredness.

In all of the work that I teach, shadow tending has always been the coursework that students are most afraid of. The biggest fear is that they will learn something about themselves that they don't want to know. In all the years that I've taught this work that has never happened, yet it remains the most dreaded coursework in my curriculum.

We have to be able to identify and work with shadow because until we do, it unconsciously speaks through us. We continue to respond in that less-grounded way until we realize that we can choose otherwise and until that opportunity to do shadow work presents itself. Shadow parts happen because at the time we didn't have the skills to respond otherwise. Now we do, and this is the crux of crafting ritual around shadow parts—tending them by giving them voice, agency. As with all tension that remains unresolved, we hand down shadows that haven't been tended.

When we get past the fear that we will learn something about ourselves that we don't want to know, we're left with the depth of our potential, which can be intimidating in its own way. If we can approach our shadows as merely aspects of ourselves that need help, skills, or a different perspective on a dynamic, it's much harder to demonize ourselves. In fact, shadows are most often child versions of ourselves who need something that the adults in our lives at that time could not give or teach us. Through shadow tending we become tasked with having compassion for ourselves and learning more mature ways of responding, which are deeply confrontational and the real reason we all fear shadow. We fear the depth of work it requires, the shift it creates in our identity—and thus the shift in how we show up in community—and the change in how we move among that it demands.

In the way that we really only greet our sacredness through heartbreak, we really only experience the strength and liberation of our shadows by being vulnerable to our darkness, by standing in the unknown of our scars. Shadow tending taps into intense vulnerability, fragility, and messiness, which require that we name or feel what hurts and articulate why. We have to be clear about what was needed that wasn't given, who didn't give it, and the toll that lack took on our ability to hold our sacredness. That healing also comes with homework. In shadow tending we become accountable to the full expression of those feelings, to those we've harmed while living out of shadow, to how we have harmed ourselves, and to learning new, healthy ways to manage life dynamics and relationships going forward. Ultimately shadow tending results in becoming reacquainted with our calling, speaking out, and punching up.

Given my formative experiences with accessing my Sacred Self, I don't approach shadow tending from a place of banishment or segregation. Rather, I offer shadow inclusion. This approach can look like the following:

- Asking a shadow that is related to a specific trigger to step forward. For example, I've worked with shadow that came from an inability to articulate myself in heated exchanges with loved ones. I thought the tension came from dissociation, so I spent a great deal of time exploring those nonlinear spaces and improving my relationship to embodiment. However, with embodiment I recognized a much younger shadow took over when those exchanges happened and that this young shadow never learned how to manage conflict.
- Learning the lore of shadow. What's its story? What did it need that it did not get? What can it receive now to feel secure and be able to learn a better way?

- Giving what shadow needs to update its lore (i.e., to feel secure and capable of different options and responses). This could literally be, "You don't have to worry about getting yelled at for missing the bus, because we can drive now" and then creating a safe ritual around the experience of driving and relationship to timing.
- Exploring where Sacred Self and shadow are in relationship. What does Sacred Self provide shadow? How do they support each other? How does each contribute to functionally responding better?
- Facilitating how they can support and inform each other. Hold space for dialogue between Sacred Self and shadow. Ask Allies to give their attention to any aspects of this relationship or exchange where needed.

Dying Well and Reconciliation

We don't talk about dying well in settler culture. Even with the non-church spiritual crowd, we operate on an assumption that a nonpartisan process automatically plays out at death to ensure we end up wherever we need to be. I suspect that it does for folx on intact animistic paths. That they have an unbroken path via cosmology held over generations that guides them at death into What Comes Next. I suspect that at some point far back in our active kinship with Nature our Ancestors had such a relationship with life and death. As someone who has done deathwork for most of my life, it's not that way now in settler culture. We don't automatically know what to do at death; thus, as animists we are responsible for knowing what we and others in our lives need to die well and for restoring the dignity of good death at a cultural level. We need certain rites and witnessing in death, so that we greet What Comes Next in the best shape possible. We need to use our earthly agency to set ourselves up for a smoother transition into spiritual options and to create avenues for surviving loved ones to grieve openly.

Dying well, from my viewpoint, requires a great deal of Dream Team engagement at various life stages and looks like this:

- Coping well with the challenge of being soul in form, among
- Understanding how we must apply our agency to our calling
- Living well, so that we bear our calling to the world in a way that it blesses ourselves and our human and nonhuman communities
- Eldering well, so that we hold the leadership roles that our communities need, and we transmit our knowledge and wisdom to the descendants
- Dying well, so that we reconcile our traumas and those of our Ancestors
- Ancestoring well, so that the descendants are witnessed and tended in their time in form

When we aren't able to live in a way that fulfills these aspects of living well, we don't die well. We become one of the unquiet dead contributing to the broken path, and for me that's a sobering thought. Thus, it bears stating that when even one of those aspects is complicated or unfulfilled at an individual's death, that knowledge should be taken into how we craft death rites, so that the soul moves on fully unencumbered.

Ideally death rites facilitate ushering the soul of the departed out of the formed experience and into the spirit realm where, when it's ready, the soul can seek reconciliation of remaining personal and ancestral trauma. Again, at some earlier point in human development that process may have been automatic, or we were so closely aligned with our cosmology and supported by human and nonhuman community throughout our lives that we didn't have to tend death and beyond as fastidiously. In settler culture neither of these rites is widely done. The result of that is many unquiet dead don't move into the spirit realm, and legacies of unreconciled ancestral trauma thrive.

We aren't going to fix that interweaving of troubled legacies with a handful of ritual potentials, though we elder well by being more cognizant of how we move among, so that we are in close, active relationship with our cosmology, and we progressively cultivate the skills to reconcile personal and ancestral trauma ongoing through life. Rituals that could facilitate timely entry into the spirit world at death look mostly like doing what facilitates us to live as a good custodian to the planet and bear our unique gift to the planet, including the following:

- Knowing intimately who we're moving among—human communities, Naturekin relationships, well Ancestors, Allies, systems, beliefs, and so on

- Tending our inner cosmology, including listening to our body, regulating our mind and emotions, and engaging our sacredness on a regular basis

- Engaging our cosmology on a regular basis through offerings, inviting help from Allies and well Ancestors, and performing divinations

- Holding space for our cosmology to shift so that who needs to come to the fore can, who needs to shift back is still honored, and new beings who need space in our sacredness can find it

- Holding willingness to tend shadow and other soul tension and fragmentation so that we are more embodied with our cosmology and capable of expressing personal trauma

- Engaging our Dream Team so they can address ancestral trauma to reconcile its personal, lineage, and collective impact

- Shaping our life as much as we can to support all of the above and using our agency to bear our unique gift

- Doing all of the above to the betterment of all life, not just for ourselves

That said, we can do all of the above and still not die well. We can live peace-filled, such that we reconcile traumas and deeply engage cosmology, yet experience a traumatic death that prevents us from moving on. We can live peace-filled lives and move on, but not reconcile our ancestral wounds, which are further handed down. It's also possible that some of us aren't capable of doing any of the above due to physical or mental disability or lack of access to such knowledge or skills. For this reason our death rites must be impeccably curated to individual needs and as much as possible take into consideration the individual's experience. If we don't meet the needs of the dead, their unrest creates imbalance in the formed world and spirit realm. When the dead are unquiet, we are all unquiet.

Deathwalking the Unquiet Dead

As I've said in many interviews and articles, receiving visitations from the dead was my first realization in childhood that I was experiencing life in a way that folx around me weren't. When I was seven years old I saw the Disney movie *Child of Glass* (based on the book *The Ghost Belonged to Me),* and that's when I realized more was being asked of me from the dead and I didn't have elders to teach me how to do it. That led to a lifelong education on all matters of death, dying, and how we can be in relationship with them.

In 1987, I found the work of Edith Fiore, Ph.D., who coined the phrase "unquiet dead" to describe those who lingered in the human realm after death and the resulting problems this stagnation creates. I didn't and don't resonate with everything Fiore presented, but her work opened a needed dialogue around death and dying that until then had not been common conversation in 1990s soul work (and frankly wasn't until the past five+ years, as of the publication of this book). The reason that a soul is unquiet is because it wasn't deathwalked out of formed being to the spirit realm, and its personal and/or ancestral trauma hadn't been reconciled. As we've noted, beings with active relationships with their cosmologies achieve movement into the spirit realm. Those without active relationships with their cosmologies do not. Regardless of relationship to cosmology, *in settler culture neither group reconciles their trauma.* Reconciliation of personal and ancestral trauma isn't part of the collective approach to death rites in settler culture.

When the dead don't have the opportunity to move on and release their trauma, it shows up in formed being. Unresolved trauma doesn't just disappear at death. It is a life force that lives on and has to go somewhere. The tension it creates shows up in different ways, some more direct than others. On a personal level, you may have a disturbance in your home—inexplicable sounds, shadows, movement. The space or land may just feel "off." Maybe you are stuck in a specific life area and can't gain traction no matter how much skill, elbow grease, prayer, healing, or energy tending you give it. Stuckness of this sort points to unresolved ancestral trauma. The life forces of stuck systemic dynamics, like poverty, racism, misogyny, are emboldened by unresolved trauma. I don't use the words *ghost* or *haunting*, though I fully concur with the suggestion of Mathias Nordvig, Ph.D., in *The Sacred Flame* episode "Ancestors: The Spirits of the Land," when he suggests that haunting is land-based anger.

We've previously talked about trauma as the key thing that separated humanity from our awareness of being Nature and as the primary reason that we don't have elders initiated into ways of tending that relationship. We've also discussed trauma as the key culprit in not having sufficient death rites. Each of these alone is a problem in terms of creating distance from our place in sacred order and as custodians of the planet. When we examine them together we're challenged to reintroduce rituals to tend our dying and dead in a way that doesn't exacerbate the long and deep cultural lack of proper death rites, and where possible, tends the backlog of unquiet dead and the ancestral wounds it has created. Because of the interwoven personal and collective aspects of dying well, rituals to tend the unquiet dead can be complex, and they require deep empathy and skill with emotional regulation. In my approach to deathwalking, these rituals include:

- Honoring the cosmology of the dead.
- Tending body, which varies by tradition. It's also important to state that our queer, trans, disabled, and BIPOC communities' bodies need a more tending than is commonly given. When our bodies have been armor, that needs its own release at death.

- Providing care and/or witnessing what is needed and engaging cosmological relationships to bring that to completion. This often is mere confirmation of death. Folx don't realize they've died and sitting with them through that realization can be enough. Some may be afraid and need escorting into the spirit world, which can occur through their cosmology or in the company of the spirits of loved ones. Others may be confused and just need help getting their bearings. They may have unfinished business in the formed world and need gentle affirmation around that or the opportunity to tie things up in order to let go.
- Restoring the energetic hygiene of the dead.
- Engaging the elements to return body back to Nature.
- Engaging the elements to reallocate life force back to Nature and/or descendants.
- Cultivating the discernment to know the timing and progression of all of the above and when to step back.
- Facilitating the grief of the living. When our grief stagnates, the dead can't move on.

Not everyone wants to demonstrate accountability to the human experience in form by deathwalking the unquiet dead, and that's okay. It isn't for everyone. However, we should all at least have a Dream Team member who does this work that we can call on when there's a need. None of the above components can be done by Allies or Ancestors. *If Spirit Allies could do deathwalking, there would be no unquiet dead.* These components of death rituals can only be done by humans. While deathwalking can be more complex, most of the above aspects of ritual around death and dying well can be engaged by anyone, and those that require deeper skill can be engaged by a Dream Team member.

Ancestor Tending

Ancestor tending is deathwalking, but instead of just being performed for an individual it's also done for a dynamic, for a collective. It's the difference between working with one thread versus the whole tapestry. An impaired thread is in relationship with the tapestry and doesn't alone carry the whole significance of the tapestry. Yet as the thread's relationship to the tapestry reveals distress, the diminished integrity of the tapestry becomes evident. As long as the condition of the full tapestry remains unaddressed, adding more thread doesn't resolve the original problem and further challenges the integrity of the whole. As well, addressing only the impaired thread doesn't restore the integrity of the whole tapestry.

The way ancestral trauma works with humans is similar. When we can identify a disruption in our present life, we can collaborate with Dream Team members to express the underlying trauma and gain skills to move among in a more functional way. We can address the thread. When we identify disruption in our personal lives as stemming from something that came before us or in our field—i.e., ancestral trauma—it's still because we've first recognized a problematic dynamic or stuckness in our own lives. The difference is that the stuckness didn't originate in our present lives; rather, we were born into an Ancestor's unexpressed trauma, which filtered through every subsequent generation. When this is the case, we must direct our care to the full wound, to the whole tapestry. Our awareness, care, and skills must stretch back across generations of Ancestors between ourselves and the one who experienced the original wound, each of whom also experienced their version of a problematic dynamic in their lives. With this weaving of multiple personal experiences into the first wound, a tapestry of compounded trauma is created. We are tasked with healing the original wound, as well as all the iterations of it experienced down to our own. Ancestor tending involves a great deal of ritual and skill that isn't typically found in a basic soul-tending skill set, though it's doable with Dream Team support.

Ancestor tending demonstrates deep understanding of accountability to All Things. It contains the pit of our unreconciled personal and systemic oppression, hatred, and violence and is the wellspring of our human strength, joy, and gifts. It is as much our job to clean up human messes to protect each other and our descendants as it is to preserve the integrity and possibility of human compassion to inspire us all. Do we owe our abusive and hateful Ancestors reconciliation? That's up to each of us to decide, really. I don't feel I owe them anything, though I do owe it to myself, my community, and my kids to make the effort to reconcile as much of our lineage trauma as I can.

My rituals around tending my Ancestors include:

- Checking in on my deceased relatives to see that they have died well and if not, giving them what's needed as I'm permitted or going to a Dream Team member to do so.
- Reconciling trauma for loved ones who have passed on but aren't fully fit to guide as Ancestors.
- Reconciling the trauma of Ancestors who are obstinate and dangerous and require Dream Team help.
- Honoring the strengths of my Ancestors with offerings, space in my Ancestor cabinet, or through song and dance.
- Honoring the struggles of my Ancestors.
- Acknowledging the harm my Ancestors caused me, my family, other humans, and nonhumans.
- Observing how I have internalized their struggles and how I am still in relationship with the harm they caused—because I am. We are. Until we do the work to reconcile that relationship, we are still in it and causing harm. Even if that harm involves systems that are enormous and beyond our control, our awareness and reconciliation of relationship to the originating harm changes how we move among now.
- Engaging my well Ancestors in conversation and seeking their guidance.

Similar to deathwalking, there is great complexity in the reconciliation of ancestral wounding and in how we are in relationship with it. It draws on many soul-tending skills and requires Dream Team collaboration. What is important for us all to do in Ancestor work is to cultivate a space for them in our cosmology, be open to how their strengths and complications show up in our lives, and be responsive to them in a way that leaves us better than we arrived here.

INTROSPECTION

Reassessing Your Place-Space Kin and Dream Team

As you begin this introspection, take time to deepen your embodiment practice, as well as learn what place-space relationships are relevant for you. Sit with those kin and feel them fully before moving on with the cultivation of diverse rituals. Let compassionate curiosity lead you in trying as many different ways as needed to find what works and hold it loosely enough to feel when different approaches are needed.

As well, reconsider your Dream Team. It's very common for our list of Dream Team members to evolve in the same way that our relationship to cosmology continues to evolve. You may find that while a Dream Team member benefitted you wonderfully in your exploration of fit elderhood, they may not align with where you are and what you need now. They may not understand who you are now. Consider the following:

❋ What needs are currently being met by your Dream Team? What ones are not? Sit with what needs aren't being met and why. Name them as explicitly as possible.

❋ If your needs have changed, how can you address this fact with your Dream Team member(s) directly?

❋ What closure might be needed around such Dream Team relationships?

❋

Preparing for Ritual

The ritual elements mentioned in this chapter are not wish-list territory. Don't engage in a ritual merely based on the order I've given. Engage in it because it's the one that genuinely best meets the most pressing needs. While the urgency in eldering is real, there's no race. There's no finish line. Our job is to do the rituals that are ours to do, fully, and we can't do that in earnest if we pressure ourselves (or feel pressured by others) to engage in a way that isn't authentic.

When it comes to grief tending, shadow tending, dying well and reconciliation, deathwalking, and Ancestor tending, we will repeat and flesh out our rituals over and over as our needs change. And even though these ritual components are important in eldering well, you don't have to be highly proficient at all of them. We're not all meant to be deathwalkers or reconcilers of our own Ancestors. What's important is that we recognize when attention in these areas is needed, and we have the relationships in place through our Dream Team to get help. Bringing our awareness to dynamics that feel stuck in our lives and applying the tools and relationships that we have to facilitate them addresses the broken path and creates new, healthy routes forward.

It's also important to remember that ritual doesn't have to be a somber, heavy undertaking. It's okay to be playful and shake up your rituals for different occasions. To prepare for ritual, consider the following:

✻ How do you call in your cosmology?

✻ What fetishes represent beings in your cosmology? Where should they be physically placed when opening sacred space?

✻ In what ways can you honor the cosmology of someone else?

✻ How do you mourn?

✻ What are your biggest fears in meeting your shadows?

✻ How comfortable are you with knowing you caused harm?

✻ How do you distinguish between your feelings and those of another being?

❋ How do you hold knowing that your Ancestors caused harm?

❋ What actions of your Ancestors do you feel responsible for?

❋ What ancestral dynamics do you see in your own life?

❋ What actions can you take to change how those ancestral dynamics affect other people? How they uphold problematic systems?

6

Honoring Our Calling
to Tend Community

Discovering Our Personal Relationship
with All Things

When people are related to you, you treat them different.
JERRY TELLO, *RECOVERING YOUR SACREDNESS*

The well-known flight attendant instruction, "Put the oxygen mask on yourself before trying to help others" is simple, wise logic that feels unintuitive in a culture that's burning to the ground. Yet, that's exactly what we have to do to have the foundation to tend community. We have to clean up our own messes, take responsibility for the healing of ourselves, family lines, and relationships, and show up to how those lingering traumas have impacted the systems we live in now. We have to craft the way of moving among that blesses our relationships, which enables us to elevate those with whom we are in relationship. Eldering well is being other-centric, with the understanding that we are always also in relationship with ourselves.

When we talk about tending community, it conjures ideas of

leadership, public speaking, guidance, conflict resolution, and decision-making. In community, elders are people who recognize needs and know how to fill them. They see where education or skills are needed and they give them. Elders demonstrate knowledge and wisdom that underlies the bonds of the community and carries forward its lore. Likewise, the community recognizes elders as trustworthy and respectable because their lived experience enables them to make good judgments for themselves and the community. They also have a track record of success with their abilities, which means they have the discipline to excel and sustain the community. In recognition of these qualities, community bestows power upon elders.

THE GRATITUDE-COMMUNITY CONNECTION

Eldering in community may include all or some of these qualities, along with others depending on the community focus. Demonstration of them may be on an as-needed, ongoing, or just-once basis. However we understand community and tending it, relationship is at the fore. We recognize that we all bring something unique to the group, which when exchanged, enriches the lives of those in the community. According to Robin Wall Kimmerer, our gifts and responsibilities are one, and thus "asking 'What is our responsibility?' is the same as asking 'What is our gift?' It is said that only humans have the capacity for gratitude. This is among our gifts."[1] If human persons have the greatest agency on the planet, as we discussed earlier, and are the only beings in form who have the capacity for gratitude, that also means *we are the only alchemy bringing those forces together.* Wyrdweaving through gratitude is our greatest magick and how we form community.

Like embodiment practices, gratitude practices have made their social media rounds, with tacked-on embellishments regarding abundance and productivity. They often emphasize the outcome of gratitude, rather than gratitude itself. When we practice true gratitude, we become more aware of how we're in relationship with the world around us—humans, Naturekin, and spirit realm. Specifically, with gratitude, we center these relationships. We bring them to the fore of our awareness of how we move among.

We can all identify and feel places in which we experience the broken path, often on a daily basis. The fracture exists—though it's maybe not always readily felt despite the fact that it underlies every other break—in not recognizing that we are inherently in community with Nature. Always. We don't have to seek it out to be so. We don't have to ask. We don't have to lead and make speeches or possess specific skills. We don't even have to ask forgiveness for not recognizing that we are kin—though it may be thoughtful to acknowledge that in some supportive ritual. We have only to experience at a deeply lived level that we are all born into the community that is Nature, to feel and act from the sense of belonging that it imparts, to understand how we will be of service to the whole, and to allow the support Nature brings us.

Rituals expressing gratitude can be as simple as giving acknowledgment, singing to our space, leaving ecologically safe offerings to Oak, Monarch, Morning, or whomever we most need to honor, or creating a gratitude shrine in a place where we spend regular time that houses fetishes of all of our most cherished relationships. Very basic, regular expression of our gratitude for what sustains us every day situates us more deeply in immediate relationship in its own right and also shapes our perspective on community. This sustained gratitude practice helps us internalize that we are a vital part of those relationships and sharpens the realization that we have something unique to give. That reciprocity, that sense of duty to our most foundational relationships to place-space, supports everything we go out and do in the world.

THE GRATITUDE-TRAUMA CONNECTION

In the early chapters of this book, we talked about trauma as the result of pain we are left alone in. We discussed that we don't honor kinship with Nature in settler culture, the root of which is collective and personal unexpressed trauma compounded by harmful current cultural systems. The work of Odelya Gertel Kraybill, Ph.D., produced a model indicating a relationship between trauma, isolation, and gratitude, which I feel also informs our ability to carry our agency in community. Kraybill's approach to trauma therapy is called the Six Stage Trauma Integration Roadmap (ETI Roadmap). These six stages are (1) routine, (2) event, (3) withdrawal, (4) awareness, (5) action, and (6) integration.

What she found while developing the ETI Roadmap was that after the traumatic event stage, a trigger lingers, resulting in "the chronic sense of danger [which] often activates a withdrawal response."[2] Such a response is a natural reaction when the nervous system feels threatened. We seek comfort, relaxation, and the chance to regulate. However, when the withdrawal response becomes an internalized, uncontrollable cycle, folx begin to cut themselves off from social engagement as the default way of being, which reinforces the loss of hope and the feelings of isolation and not being good enough. This dynamic eventually results in a sense of not belonging and arrests the brain function that allows us to experience gratitude. It suggests a dynamic in which we can't help but feel alone. *This effect means that trauma literally interferes with our ability to bear the human gift of gratitude and thus with our ability to situate into community.* This means that trauma directly interferes with our ability to use our gifts and agency as humans. While carrying unexpressed trauma, we can't do what we were built to do here.

In response to this biological and social trauma dynamic, Kraybill deduced that trying to change how we feel reinforces the overriding sense that something is wrong, which reengages the withdrawal response. So instead of trying to change our feelings, her ETI Roadmap focuses on awareness, which is being present and embodied, as the felt sense that shifts us out of withdrawal. She goes on to state that when we can feel compassion for ourselves, we can expand our capacity to cope not because we are grateful for our traumatic experiences but because through self-awareness and compassion we are able to feel what we feel without judging ourselves for having those feelings, which allows us to expand our capacity for them.[3]

Kraybill's work centers on the individual's experience of trauma and how it impacts their capability to feel gratitude. As animists, we can also honor that it describes our cultural relationship to gratitude. As a generations-long traumatized people challenged in expressing and engaging gratitude, we are left withdrawn and disengaged from our Nature community.

And that's not our fault. It isn't our fault that we fell out of awareness of our kinship with Nature as an ancestral withdrawal stance. It isn't our fault that we haven't been able to heal generations-old neurological trauma responses or override deep cultural imperatives that have further held us apart from Nature, because part of what was lost were our cultural rituals to do exactly that. As well, it isn't our fault that we couldn't overcome the deep shame, anger, and injury at our realization that we had lost awareness of this relationship.

Yet our challenge in this dynamic is to realize that by collectively stalling in the withdrawal stance, we perpetuate the cycle of harm, and we must choose to move differently. We must choose awareness as a route through to action and integration, to a new path to Nature relationship. Our challenge in this trauma dynamic is, as Kraybill suggests, not to change how we feel or think about it but to observe it and feel it and allow that information to come forward through us, *through our embodiment.*

When we can give that space to an expression of pain, we can expand our capacity to feel joy, which permits us access to gratitude.[4] As well, it allows us to respond differently to the pressure to remain broken and begin the ancestral and community healing that's needed. The relationship between trauma, gratitude, and community is Dream Team territory. In that lifelong work we find our worth to community and bear our gifts forward as fit elders.

NATURE COMMUNITY

Author Charles Vogl states the draw of community well when he says that we value what we put our "warm bodies" near.[5] He goes on to say that criteria such as shared values, membership identity, moral proscriptions, insider understanding, and serving members are qualities that healthily functioning communities uphold. The bottom line in his wisdom of a good community is that no member can feel left out or untended. These are all excellent components of a strong community that could also be ways of expressing that healthy communities share some core relationship to cosmology. They don't necessarily have the same cosmology and aren't in relationship with cosmology in the same way, but they are capable of making space for diverse cosmology relationship to happen, regardless.

Typically, we think of community as a group that's come together based on shared interests, goals, or vicinity. In that framework, human-centered community conveys more as an extracurricular activity that we do on weekends or some set interval, such as performing a civic duty, going to church, or playing board games. We dip in and out of it as compelled. It may denote a hierarchical organization or be a total free-for-all, though it usually still comprises class-based involvement in which some folx are leaders, inner-ring members, or beginners. Our cultural observation of community doesn't necessarily convey "a group of individuals who share a mutual concern for one another's welfare."[6]

From the vantage point of tending the broken path, how do we value Nature by where we place our warm bodies? How do we hold space for recognition that Nature has always been concerned for our welfare? How does our awareness of that fact affect how we bear our agency in the world? How do we conduct our human community relationships well when we're disjointed from our awareness of place in Nature? I don't think we can, which means we also can't fully express trauma in a supportive human community or fully bear our unique gift. I've experienced in my own soul exploration that where I limit vulnerability and intimacy with human persons is also where I limit them with nonhuman persons. This is also ultimately true of our cultural relationship with Nature.

NATURE COSMOLOGY

As with cosmology, if we aren't born into a human community that healthily holds us, it is difficult to find one in settler culture. It's also no accident that both cosmology and community are often inextricably linked through organized religion. Despite growing up on the outskirts of a small town with only my mother and sister, I had an enormous extended family, most of whom lived in proximity to each other. The aunts, uncles, cousins, grandparents, great aunts, great uncles, great-grandparents that I saw on every holiday and Sunday lunch were the same ones I saw on Sunday mornings at church, Sunday evenings at youth studies, Wednesday at choir practice, and in Girl Scouts—for all of my childhood. These were the people who brought the casseroles after funerals and the ones who gave rides when the car was in the shop. Every aspect of my spiritual community was bound into birth family. The lack of community outside of family made it very hard to leave the church when I realized I needed to listen to my own spiritual wisdom as a late teen. I knew that parting from that church community would be parting with some family members.

In settler culture, it's common to be handed cosmology at birth with no regard as to whether it actually meets our needs or anyone's needs. Whether it's from our birth family or the wider social systems built on supremacy that support our livelihood, we are all born into human community with cosmologies at their center that have at best not supported us and at worst caused us harm. We also have to explore that by being in such communities, we have possibly caused harm—to ourselves, other humans, and Naturekin. These facts, coupled with the difficulty of locating human community that can support us, become their own shadows that must be tended.

This entanglement of wounding in human community and thus cosmology leaves us with hurt to work through. We have to confront that work so that we can come into deep relationship with our cosmology in such a way that we can access it fluidly with rituals, respect the cosmology of others without trying to take or change them, and find and emulate the common values that our cosmology shares with others. In order to do what we came here to do and die well, we need active, engaged relationship with cosmology. If we can't do that through a known cosmology, we have to continue to refine our own.

As well, we can't just throw out root cosmologies that no longer suit us. Erasure is shadow. We can't pretend those relationships didn't happen and that we didn't shape ourselves and our lives around them. We also don't have to continue supporting them. We can treat them like compost—root experiences and relationships that supported us in finding our own relationship to cosmology and continuing to do so as we grow.

Likewise, we have to see where we're in relationship with unhealthy cosmologies that we can't just withdraw from, not just ones that harmed us individually, but ones that continue to harm collectives. For example, colonization is part of our cosmology, whether we consciously approve of it or rail against it, it has power over us. We have to determine how we're in relationship with it and make choices in how we live.

In chapter 2, I observed a component of cosmology across walks of students and clients that may be useful to return to in exploring and healing relationship to Naturekin and human community. When I've asked folx to whom they felt most connected in childhood, they named animals, trees, and sitting spots outdoors. Coming back to these pivotal relationships and exploring how they can expand is an entryway back into awareness of Self as Nature and Self as already in community with All Things.

SACRED PARENTS

We traverse the fragility of our relationship to our collective past through willing vulnerability. Until we craft viable ways to sit with our vulnerability, we remain locked in the cycle of forgetting who we are. Until we remember who we are, we remain uncomfortable with vulnerability. But who teaches us to find our way in that relationship in settler culture? Who teaches us that we are made of vulnerability stitched together with courage and hope?

Ideally, our parents teach us. Our family and community elders teach us. Unfortunately for most of us on the broken path, that's not where we learn to embrace all aspects of who we most deeply are. We learn it from heartbreak and trauma, sometimes at the hands of our parents or other trusted elders or from our trusted adults not responding supportively to harm that was done to us by others. When we don't have fit elders to model how to navigate difficulty, we can balk at the idea of becoming elders ourselves. We can only see the route to maturity as becoming our own abusers, and quite possibly consuming the power of our children. We can reach a stalemate in envisioning ourselves as elders in much the same way we do with awareness in trauma. In other words, we can't envision it at all. We can't get past the trauma resulting from our own lack of mature adults to hold space for us to find and allow all the processes within us that are required to become good elders to our descendants.

I have my own legacy of heartbreak and trauma at the hands of my elders, and those experiences played a pivotal role in my hesitation to see myself as an elder. What I have learned on that very long path is that the end game of humaning is fit elderhood. If we live long enough to come to our own realization of where and how we elder, that *is* the sacred order of being human. It's coming, whether I set myself up for it or run screaming from it. The more I can return to what I came here to do and *do it*, the less I'm derailed by fears of what I might become as the result of ignorance, chromosomes, or blind fate.

The thing is, our parents' parents didn't teach them how to elder well either and neither did their parents and so on for generations back. Yes, to heal that dynamic of elders fractured from kinship with Nature is an excellent intention to bring into Ancestor tending. Likewise, it may not be possible for us to come to a peaceful place with our birth family, where our trauma, vulnerability, and personal version of elderhood are concerned. There remains the fact that we weren't intended to do any of this alone. If we don't have the people who birthed us into being moving among with us, who else is left?

Ourselves, foremost. We can, through diverse Dream Team support and education, learn to express childhood needs and trauma, such that we see and accept the sacred authority in parenting ourselves. We can validate the children of our inner cosmology by acknowledging the sources of their pain and who caused it. We can demonstrate compassion for ourselves by creating and managing our own boundaries. And in a valiant act of vulnerability, we can widen our awareness of our ecosystem and community to feel how we are situated in a greater web of support and compassion.

That web may include ancestral support. Even though we talk a lot about ancestral tending, it's not always easy to do. If our relationship with our immediate family was problematic or harmful, it's hard to conceive of reaching beyond them into the family lines that created them or to understand why that stretch is needed. Often when doing ancestral work with folx, the well Ancestors who initially come are from *way back,* well before the regime of settler culture, before indigeneity was threatened. They're from early lineages who functioned as conduits into belonging. This means they weren't perfect beings who lived romantic lives in harmony with Nature but seasoned elders who made mistakes and persevered through hardship to resurrect themselves as rooted resources on what it means to be human. These are the Ancestors who know what time it is and have elected to teach us now. Engaging them is an empowering route into regulation around parents and parenting Self.

We've talked about Naturekin and Spirit Allies as supporters who, through their own agency whisper to ours, give us motivation, momentum, and foundation. They are certainly family, though they don't necessarily fill the role of parent. They don't impart that felt sense of rooted caretaking of the earthly experience or have access to informed direction on a dynamic or possibility. However, we do have access to what parented all of form into being. To be deeply heard, seen, and held, I turn to our Sacred Parents—Earth Parent and Sky Parent—who are our first Ancestors and whom others have referred to as Celestial Parents or First Parents.

For some they are gendered, as in Mother Earth or Father Sky, though in my experience of them, their gender shifts. They may be deities for some folx. Likewise, I experience that their representation in number varies. Sometimes I experience Sky Parent, sometimes it's Sky Family. What's important is being open to how they come into our sacred space, coming into our own direct personal relationship with them, and letting the details of those relationships grow with experience.

I could feel and engage Earth Parent for many years before I could comfortably approach Sky Parent. I would meet my Sacred Earth Family in an underworld cave space from which we'd take long walks, sit by a creek, or hug for a few fleeting moments. Those interactions gave me a felt sense of connection from my lower abdomen into the ground, which I can call on any time to more deeply root and anchor my embodiment. With Earth Parent I find an extension of my lore into a timeless story of creation and relationship that both teaches and affirms me.

Sky Parent was a different story. Divesting this Ancestor of religious overtones, patriarchal projections, and gendered binary was really important for me to begin cultivating this relationship. When I could heal my relationship to this Ancestor, it came through in a very clear, gentle, yet enthusiastic sense of being held. This Parent situates as a collective atop a fluffy cloud beyond Earth Soul. When I engage their space my connection comes in the relaxation of my body, a distinct quiet in my mind, and a feeling of being anchored into a version of myself that existed long before my body, while folded in a reverence for physicality that I don't often feel in body, in my day-to-day.

Perhaps it goes without saying that greeting these Celestial Ancestors will likely come with heartache, vulnerability, and accountability. As with aspects of soul relationship we've already discussed, our happiness and relief are most often met with tension and the revelation of more work. For me working with Celestial Parents brought up deeply buried feelings of not trusting the multiverse, not believing that my needs would (or could) be met, and feeling not enough. Just because I could recognize them as my oldest Ancestors didn't mean I could readily receive what they had to offer. Those relationships remain works in progress for me. What they've brought me despite my hesitation to be intimate with them is the full circle of kin, from the far reaches of the multiverse across time, to neighbors, people I don't know on the other side of the planet, my own gut biome, and the moss that grows in the crevice where my grass meets my driveway.

When we engage our Sacred Parents, we're not bypassing our issues with our earthly parents. In fact, when we hold our full progression into form, our parents are part of the lineage from our Sacred Parents, by default. We're not omitting them or ignoring their impact on our lives. We're not denying the internalized traumas that they handed down to us. Rather, by engaging our Sacred Parents, we are extending a new avenue of our own elderhood and pattern breaking.

In truth, even if we had an awesome relationship with our earthly parents, there's a point in our maturation where we realize we can't turn to them to fill our needs anymore and that we shouldn't. That point in settler culture can feel very unsupported, as if we're stepping out into nothing. We know we don't have all of the information and direction we need, yet that support has to come from somewhere.

I see this step as a point of self-initiation, one in which we can turn to our Sacred Parents. When we can grow away from our earthly parents as our primary caregivers—good, bad, or indifferent—and become caregivers for ourselves, we allow our parents to focus on themselves. By doing so we unburden them—regardless of whether they could meet our needs—and step into taking responsibility for our continued growth and direction. We take responsibility for how we move among as a human person through direct relationship with our Sacred Parents and by doing so begin to step into our elderhood and walk more deeply into ourselves as Naturekin. We begin to move with mutual awareness, respect, and responsibility.

Many rituals may be appropriate for this transition. We may need to deathwalk an aspect of ourselves who clings to parental direction, despite knowing that direction is no longer appropriate for who we are. There may be more than one aspect who needs this kind of attention. We may need to validate and call forward our Self parent through a blessing ritual. We may need to reconcile unexpressed anxiety, anger, or fear around readiness to become an elder or around our parents' inability to elder us the way we wanted or needed. Most definitely we can invite and welcome in the Sacred Parents, introduce ourselves to them, and create ways to honor them in our everyday lives.

Celestial Parents are the elders of Nature, as we know it. The ability to live into our connectedness with them, with Nature, is acknowledgment of our first family. It is our first community and holds our most foundational, educational, and transformational teachings. When we can situate ourselves within this first community at the forefront of our relationship with other humans and the spirit realm, we are coming into relationship with ourselves as fit elders.

INTROSPECTION

Exploring Your Ancestor and Naturekin Communities

As you approach this introspection, engage your embodiment practice and current place-space relationships. As you hold in mind your experience and felt sense of community with Nature, consider the following:

❋ Have you grieved the tools, rituals, and cosmology that weren't handed down to you?

❋ Have you grieved the pain of those that were that caused harm?

❋ If you engage in soul travel or other means of communicating with Ancestors, how do they describe community?

☀ How does their perspective of community compare to yours?

☀ In what ways did they tend community that could be helpful for you?

☀ In what ways did they tend community that were harmful? In what ways does that harm manifest now in your life? In current collective systems?

☀ What do your immediate Naturekin express around being family with you? What do they need from you? From their vantage point, what is respectful engagement between yourself and them?

☀ How are the ecosystems of your body in relationship with those of your immediate Naturekin?

☀ What seasonal attributes affect how you connect with the ecosystems of your place-space?

☀ In what ways does your relationship with immediate Naturekin mirror how you are in relationship with human persons? In what ways does it contradict how you are in relationship with human persons? To what do you attribute that distinction?

Greeting Your Sacred Parents

Take time to sit with the idea of Sacred Parents, paying close attention to thoughts, feelings, beliefs, and memories that stir.

☀ How does the mind respond when you think of Sacred Parents?

☀ How does body respond when you think of them?

☀ How do your mind and body respond when you think of your own family and parents?

☀ Does thinking of Sacred Parents as Ancestors change any of the above responses?

As it feels doable, greet your Sacred Parents. They may already occupy space in your cosmology. Perhaps they were there, though you didn't recognize them as such. Perhaps even as you sit with the possibility of meeting them, you feel aspects of your cosmology rising to support that meeting. It's possible to meet them by asking trusted beings in your cosmology to lead you to them or to bring a felt sense of them into your body. Note that greeting them both at once may be overwhelming. If so, try greeting them one at a time.

7
Passing on Our Lore with Compassion

Valuing Our Unique Gift Enough to Give It

A society grows great when old men plant trees whose shade they know they shall never sit in.

GREEK PROVERB

Undaunted care and awareness may bring us in closer relationship to our sacredness, our human community, our immediate Naturekin and ecosystem, our well Ancestors, and our unquiet dead. Thoughtful rebellion and well-placed wrath may outcreate harmful systems and lay the groundwork for human communities that teach, challenge, and hold us accountable. What sustains all communities can only be love and compassion. They create the foundation for us to stand on and help us hold supportive space for each other. Before we can give to community with intention, we have to understand that there's no such thing as self-work; rather, it's agency spent that reverberates through and impacts community, over and over. For that impact to have integrity it must be brought forward lovingly and compassionately for all. The bottom line is we have to value our gift and bear it to community, and to do that we must have empathy.

THE COMMUNAL HEART

Awareness of interrelationship is what enables us to have empathy for each other, to take care of each other. However, to deeply situate our empathy, our perspective of interdependence has to span beyond human-centric awareness. We have to expand our view of where we stand, which isn't just among *now*. Interdependence stretches beyond our engagement of an interagential all-community now to human person, multispecies, place-space, and spiritual communities of the past, which sets us up for thoughtfully tending community of the present and creates the same for future. We are in relationship with all of it, right now and ongoing.

Just as being gifted in form grants human persons advantage in agency, so does interdependence. When we are all taken care of and have a sense of belonging and trust, we become unstoppable forces whose collective agency functions in solidarity. We become able to create, or outcreate, in solidarity. With that expanded vantage point and range of impact, we have to begin behaving with interagency in mind. We have to craft the technologies of our cultural success not just for our own benefit but for the blessing of those who came before us and for the benefit of those among us now and those who will come after us. This expanded range of vision, this experience of Self in direct personal relationship, is the difference between adulting and eldering well. It's the difference between having rituals and cosmology and engaging rituals to situate relationship in cosmology over and over, to deepen the relationship to the tools themselves—what they allow us to access, and what they allow us to accomplish.

When we move among without internalizing engaged relationship with cosmology and place-space, when we don't grok that our cosmology already brushes against and overlaps into those of others, we're functioning as an individual. We're not moving among as animists aware that we are already in relationship, already having an impact. As my teacher, Bayo Akomolafe says, "Your story's already a matter of public concern."[1]

Because we are not separate from our immediate ecosystem, neither are our rituals or cosmologies. They are the engagement of our relationship with each other and with the ecosystem, elements, directions, Allies, Ancestors, Spirits of Place—all of it, as needed. Our inner cosmology is connected to how we make sense of and engage the world around us, that wider cosmology that holds all of those relationships for us, and is in relationship with other cosmologies. And that is as intended.

I've studied with folx on indigenous paths who have had cosmology handed down to them, unbroken, and with the mandate that that cosmology shouldn't be changed. It should be static and in that time-tested consistency inherently capable of handling change that arises. I can see how this would be true of a generations-old collective of place-space and spirit relationships. Such is a truly special and powerful kindred, which many folx in settler culture can't experience. As such, we often don't know our ancestral cosmologies and can't know them. We are still forming healthy, ethical relationship with place-space, while reaching back to reclaim ritual and lore that wants to walk with us on different land. We are culling the overculture cosmology and learning what in it isn't supportive, how we're in relationship with it, and how we move forward with our legacies and current place-spaces in a way that benefits our communities. For us, this evolution hinges on observation, respect, and the cultivation of strong spiritual technologies.

Cosmology is inherently interdependent, thus interagential. It provides the safe foundation from which we engage our agency/wyrdweave. When we're strong in our ecosystem and spirit relationships, we better apply our agency. When we apply our agency well, we strengthen those relationships and act from interagency. Working intentionally through cosmology acknowledges inherent relationship and the role those relationships play in the weaving. The way that our cosmology expands and allows us to adapt our agency to meet our needs is the same way that we grow: by experiencing life and relationships, which is to say, by experiencing change.

Because we are inherently participating in ecosystems and communities, our spiritual technologies can't just meet our personal needs. They have to be able to support the needs of our place-space and time, which means they also must meet the needs of our present ecosystem and community, and beyond.

We are here to share our knowledge. Part of why we go through everything we do is to impart that experience and wisdom to the descendants, so that they don't have to repeat our mistakes, they can stay connected to lineage lore, and they can draw on that knowledge to make the best choices amidst challenges in their lives. That means our soul tech—our lore—must have the flexibility to be handed down and adapted to the needs and ecosystems of our descendants.

We have to teach the descendants what we know but also how to identify when those technologies aren't meeting the need, and how to adapt them so that they will. In doing so, we hold space for the descendants to craft their own rituals that evolve shared cosmology, such that the soul tech can shift in a way that maintains the integrity of its boundaries, while still fulfilling its jobs under the new criteria. Then we model the work of living into the changed way of moving among with adaptive ritual, expanding cosmology.

I've heard this step into inclusive elderhood called many things: Collective Self, Communal Self, Communal Heart, Oneness. It is the lived awareness not just that we are in relationship as we move among but also *behaving* in a way that blesses the relationships and the movement. It is walking what we talk, among. *If there is a singular stride that must be exemplified in eldering well, it's living into the Communal Heart, and it can happen at any age.* Eldering well is being othercentric, with the understanding that we are always in relationship. But how do we find our Communal Heart? How do we live through it, particularly when we haven't had elders to model it for us?

EMPATHY AND LORE

The most powerful technologies we have to hand down to the descendants are in our lore, and the way we hand them down is through empathy. The same way that our Ancestors hold space across time and realms to advise us, we, as elders, are charged to do so for the descendants. Empathy is the gateway to relationship. It is the connecting point of community, which not only leads us into deeper awareness but allows us to create lore based on our place-space relationships.

Across cultural traditions, building lore is essential to being a good elder. In *Sand Talk*, Tyson Yunkaporta says, "The only way to store data long term is within relationship—deep connections between generations of people in custodial relation to a sentient landscape, all grounded in a vibrant oral tradition."[2] That sounds a lot like a cosmology. For folx in settler culture, this means part of how we build our soul tech requires that we build good lore by reconciling our shit and allowing the story of reconciliation its own place in the lore.

To be healthily situated in any community, we have to be empathetic. We have to move among in a way that evokes and offers understanding and compassion. *Empathy* is defined as "the action of understanding, being aware of, being sensitive to, and vicariously experiencing the feelings, thoughts, and experience of another of either the past or present without having the feelings, thoughts, and experience fully communicated in an objectively explicit manner." It is also defined as the capacity for the aforementioned, as well as "the imaginative projection of a subjective state into an object so that the object appears to be infused with it."[3] And there it is—we have empathy for animals, fictional characters, thoughts, rocks, shadow, and Self.

Let's sit with that a bit. Empathy as the ability to have compassion for ourselves means that we don't become paralyzed by judging ourselves when we make mistakes. It is the ability to feel good about ourselves without that good feeling stemming from belittling others. Empathy is, likewise, the ability to put Self in the place of another or to identify with what someone else is feeling. In other words, empathy creates or expresses a connection between beings. It is what binds relationships and roots us into them for growth.

The way we build empathy is to engage beings—particularly those different from ourselves—by listening to their stories, observing their (and our own) body responses as they speak, and responding to what we learn from listening. We can't build empathy in isolation, which is a direct result of the radical individualism of settler culture. As long as we believe the lie that we are separate from Nature, we can also believe that we are separate from nonhumans, spirits, and wyrd, which also means that we can't empathize with them or ourselves. When we live without empathy we use our agency to uphold settler culture.

Settler culture isn't just a way of moving among external systems but also among internal systems. It's how we've become wired, which doesn't challenge us to engage people or species different from ourselves with empathy, which also means that it doesn't challenge us to change what we think about beings different from ourselves. If anything, settler culture reinforces confirmation bias and that we isolate and demonize beings who are different from us. Isolation and hive mind are so deeply ingrained that we don't realize we're shaping our lore from them, even as well-intending animists. We don't realize these wirings are part of overculture cosmology.

LORE SHAPING

How we shape our lore matters in how we elder. Our lore is what reflects our relationships. It describes who we are to them and how we show up in them. In order to be really clear in those connections, we have to know who we are, for ourselves. We can't change the aspects of our wiring groomed to sabotage interdependence and empathy without knowing our own sacredness. As well, we're not likely to change that wiring at all. Rather, we continually observe how we're in relationship with it and continuously expand our capacity of how to be in that relationship differently.

To live through our sacredness we must confront shadow parts and bias that support division, which requires that we have empathy for ourselves. Until we embody ourselves and learn skills to do so among the hardships of our culture—our own hardships and cultural trials and witnessing those of others—we can't serve community as fit elders or do the work that intimacy requires. Until then, we also don't define and contribute our lore.

Likewise, in the way we can't view our cosmology as personal, we can't view our lore as merely our own. True, it organizes itself in a way that speaks directly to us, though it is not merely our own. Even as we work hard to meet and sustain lore in settler culture, we have to realize that those stories root into something larger. As with empathy, in order for us to continue growing, to continue experiencing the greater relationships in which we move, we must realize how our stories overlap into other stories. We must engage people with different lore from our own. Not to take what they have. Not to move into their spiritual spaces or cosmologies. Not to push our cosmology or lore on them. But to understand how our spiritual spaces are already in relationship with theirs on a much bigger scale and that relationship between them also informs our lore. When we put our warm bodies in new place-spaces, liminal haunts, and human communities, we evolve, as does our cosmology, wisdom, and lore.

Separation from awareness of Nature kinship and radical individuality root in the same soil that believes we have nothing in common and nothing to offer community. It dwells in that paralyzed gratitude-trauma withdrawal we talked about in chapter 6. Throughout this book I've spoken of elderhood as a spiritual, cultural, and social requirement, as part of our calling as human persons to become fully fledged in carrying out our agency to benefit community. I've talked about the historical layers that created the culture that would have us continue disavowing the path, the ways we've been taught to uphold the brokenness of awareness without realizing it. We've delved into the tension of who gets to be an elder and when, and how we can locate our sacredness and grounding into the ecosystems, Allies, and Ancestors who walk with us throughout life. Of all of these complications in humaning, the biggest obstacle to stepping into elderhood is us. It is overcoming our indoctrination into systems that keep us separated from Nature community.

The most difficult challenge to overcome in eldering well is valuing that we have something to give and giving it in a way that does not center on ourselves. It isn't very difficult to figure out what we bring the planet. When we can shake off our fear of living our deepest longings and allow them expression in the world through our agency to bless All Things, we are doing what we came here to do.

Most people know what it is, though doing it in a way that isn't self-serving is less common. Living our gift in a way that only blesses ourselves is upholding the break. In an interrelated holism, that's not enough. In settler culture we're inundated with opportunities to put ego first and be rewarded with false praise when we do and not at all recognize that's what is happening. Making the choice to be aware of how we apply our agency in community and to draw on our sacredness and anchor into our Naturekin and Sacred Parent roots are unifying steps into more than who we have been taught that we are.

That said, just knowing our calling isn't enough; we have to also be able to deliver it. We have to know how to apply it in a way that meets the needs of our ecosystem and community and that may require that we learn skills to shape our calling for delivery. Moving among in this way is accepting empathy as a way of being, as application of the agency of the Communal Heart. Learning to do so based on the needs of our place-space is actively living out of that interrelationship and interagency. When we step embodied into our other-than-human relationships, we are gift-bearing and lore-shaping.

LORE SHARING

I often work with clients and students seeking guidance in how to apply their agency in some facet of soul tending who say, "I don't plan to work with humans." Which is fine. We're not all called to work directly with human persons. Some of us work with animal persons or tree persons or dynamics (also persons) of specific ecosystems. Inevitably though, when I ask, "To whom are you going to pass on your soul tending wisdom and knowledge?" I get a heavy sigh and an expression of distress regarding the human community.

When we exclude humans from how we bear our unique gift, we are essentially excluding ourselves, and thus the gift, the responsibilities of being a human person in form. It truly is fine not to center the work we do here on humans, though we can't exclude them either. We can't exclude *any* persons because we are already in relationship with them. The most often stated reason I hear from those who don't want to work with humans is because they have been hurt by them and most often while in community. To elder well we have to examine where we carry unexpressed trauma not just in specific human relationships but with human persons, in general, and do that repair work.

As the custodians of this reality, we are charged not just to carry on what we are taught from our elders and Ancestors and other teachers of our time, we also are charged to be aware of the teachings themselves *as persons*, life forces. In settler culture, it's likely that we don't know our lineage lore; thus, part of our job is to explore what our lore is and needs to be, so that life force can situate into community healthily. Lore is alive and vital, and to be sustained it must be carried on. It must be transmitted to other invested folx, to the descendants, who will engage and adapt it as needed.

Awareness of our inherent relationship with All Things isn't just personally supportive and necessary to the success of our Naturekin, it also includes our relationship to our own wisdom and knowledge and seeing that wisdom and knowledge as having their own agency. We must see ourselves as the vehicle through which they carry themselves forward. Hosting our lore is another way that we live and create global being that blesses all. It is another way we live into the Communal Heart. In fact, for many intact cultures, the ability to hand down lore is a hallmark of eldering well. It is stepping up to relationship with the technology to foster it to live beyond our time here.

LORE AND COMMUNITY

Remember that lore is the bridge between us and the mythic, our Ancestors, and the spirit world. Lore is meant to change. It is meant to be touched by the agency of each generation, each being, each body, and crafted to encompass the needs of the time. That said, holding space for our evolving lore isn't without complication. In settler culture, the story of where we come from has been hijacked and retrofitted to a whitewashed narrative of imperialism. It contains things we don't like about ourselves, our people, and our relationships, as well as unreconciled pain. We hold the story of where we come from with trepidation, even as we continue to act out that story in community. We simultaneously ignore it while feeling threatened to function differently within it.

Our lore can contain shadows, just as we do. It contains violence and scars. Just as we don't exorcise our shadow parts but care for them as part of our whole, we can't bypass the parts of our story that we don't like or that have caused harm. The same way that shadows are scars in our inner cosmology, outdated lore leaves scars in how we move among. We can't remove the scar, though we can stand in it and feel into its connective stretch to the possibility beyond it.

We engage shadow lore and learn where it isn't true for us anymore. We see where it isn't safe for ourselves or others, and we tend it without glorifying it, without pathologizing it. We engage shadow lore as the being that it is and deathwalk it to its next chapter. If salvageable, we present its scarred remains to the story of our present and invite it to move among with us in a supportive way that meets our needs and the needs of our lore and our communities.

In this way we take responsibility for our harmful lore and from those shadow narratives create something more suitable for our time. We give the narratives space to heal and to choose to move forward with us in a way that holds us all.

Eventually we realize that the shadow truths we have to confront in our personal lineages are the same truths we face collectively, culturally. They are in relationship. And without those confrontations, our lore doesn't evolve to hold us. When it doesn't evolve, we don't connect. When we don't connect, we continue to break the path.

As with generalized trauma, realizing our wounds around community also helps us to acknowledge where we have withdrawn, not just from community but from our lore, our wisdom. Our pain points to where we are vulnerable and lack confidence in sharing our lineage lore and how we avoid going where it is leading us on our spiritual path. When we can hold the painful wounds of past community and those of wider systems that we can't just step out of alongside the yearning for spiritual kinship among human persons, we create a potential for gratitude and possibility, valuing our own wisdom, and understanding what we bring to community.

When we understand how we hone our lore, we, by sheer virtue of how we carry ourselves, cultivate spaces of belonging for others. We, by the strength of how we move among, foster growth around us and cultivate accountability. We, in the way that we embody ourselves, are dependable, and thus we enrich interdependence. And if there is a starting point in how we arrive at being a good elder in human community, it's in learning how to be a good member of our Nature community.

LORE AND GRIEF

When we start to sit with our lore, how we got from where we were to where we are, all things considered, we are forced to confront where we lacked leadership, where we didn't have good elders, where we didn't receive formative lore or support in crafting our own. We come face-to-face with the grief of having to become something that wasn't modeled for us. We don't just age into elderhood, we initiate into it, and in broken-path settler culture we do not have such community-held or witnessed initiations. We have not had elders intentionally moving among their place-space relationships, applying their agency for the support of all in those spaces, weaving lore to guide us to do the same. The isolation and loneliness that characterizes American settler culture leaves us not just outside of community, but without the skills to know how to exist in community. It deprives us from learning how to be good community.

As a result, our skills for such have been learned "on the job," through trial and error, often in community, and we've made huge mistakes. We yearn for community though don't follow through with reciprocity. We seek legitimization of learned authority without recognizing the delicate balance and power of community. We strive for stabilization of our personal resources without acknowledging the ecosystems and communities they come from or the lore of how they got to us. We stretch for expansion of our spiritual awareness without thought to who we're bumping into. We run headlong toward a projection of perfection that didn't exist for us and isn't possible to create, all of which has nothing to do with eldering well. Rather, it's a colonized trauma response to radical individualism.

Facing the grief of not having had fit elders is part of settler culture initiation into elderhood. It is often an unspoken pressure we feel every step of our lives, from the point that we realize we have to elder ourselves. The scar of not having had fit elders is the yearning to be one, with the fear that we never will be. However, that scar is the pivotal connector to our relationship with community, lore, cosmology, and our agency. As long as we don't acknowledge that scar, we can't live into our unique version of eldering well that it connects us to.

I imagine the journey into becoming a well elder starts in childhood, and through community-held rites of passage we grow from child to adult to elder, throughout which we also grow as a being realizing ongoing responsibility situated in ecosystem and community. In broken-path settler culture, rather than being initiated into elderhood at the trusted hands of those who hold us, we stumble through rites of heartbreak, juggling the demands of our lives and creating lore that withstands longevity at the same time.

When I express this to folx just beginning animism or soul-tending studies, it comes out more like this: Without human community support, we are discerning supportive cosmology and cultivating the rituals to access that cosmology, while learning to embody, tend, and honor Self in community and place-space, while paying the bills, showing up for loved ones, and regulating amongst systems working against our success with all of the aforementioned every day, all day, all at once, conceivably alone. It's not just a lot. It's thousands of years of overwhelming isolation and lack and a facet of collective shadow for which we each must find a pathway into Ally. The holding of grief regarding lack of fit elders is one of the deepest wounds of our time, and while it is best served with a diversely skilled Dream Team, there are many ways we might meet the grief of not having had fit elders.

The most effective ritual I've done to express this grief was to listen to my Ancestors' stories of elderhood. Initially and as ever, when I opened the space, I was moved by how luminous, staid, and driven they were in their conviction to steward me into elderhood. I prepared myself to hear how hard human life was for them, stories of what they'd had to transmute to survive. And yes, some of them communicated a challenging yet consciously led and held living into elderhood, while others experienced quite isolated, painful journeys.

What surprised me was that first and foremost all of them recalled their lore, the wisdom of what they'd learned. While they didn't hide their tribulations that brought wisdom, they also didn't emphasize their experience of hardship to transmutation or the dire circumstances they worked to bear their unique gift. They shared their stories and how they had chosen to be in relationship with them.

Not whitewashing, not bypassing but including it all as their legacy to me.

And I sobbed. I sobbed for their celebration of me, for life, for relationship. I sobbed for how lovingly they opened themselves to beauty and vibrancy in difficulty, and how it was not one bit contrived. I sobbed for the space they made specifically to convey to me what lies on the other side of the consuming grief of what I didn't have, and how I might become that in my time here.

LORE AND BEYOND

We have to compassionately imagine our way back into the story of ourselves, of our ecosystems, of our communities. Because when we come back to the seed of sacred order that we all carry on some level, we realize those stories are inseparable, they overlap, and they hold us. They always have. When we experience ourselves in the grand narrative, it is the point where lore ceases to be merely a utility handed down to us—harmful or supportive—and becomes the point where we are *our* story, which must then be shaped by our own hands. We are our lore.

In this way eldering well isn't about leading community in the hierarchical way we've been taught but about becoming active in our lore's shape, unfolding, and transmission as wisdom, which is a precious thing to accomplish in a lifetime, in a lineage.

This unfolding of our lore isn't something that just happens in settler culture. We have to ask for it from our deepest sacredness, our Ancestors, our Allies, our ecosystem. Then we must make room for it to move of its own volition and agency in our lives and meet it with humility, curiosity, and skill to let it lead.

When we can stand in our shifting cosmology and remain committed and open to new relationships, we don't get distracted by every shiny spiritual interest or cultural seduction. To paraphrase something I've heard my teacher Christina Pratt say several times, "It's soul versus desire, and soul must win."

When we are in strong relationship with our soul tech, we become focused on what supports our growth and builds our lore, which is the story of how we adapt our lineage experience to apply our agency in our time here. It is our wisdom of how we brought our gift, wrapped in just enough teaching and possibility for the descendants to decode and tell their own. Eventually we have to realize that's what it's all about. We don't give meaning to our lives; others do. What we accomplish here, our legacy, isn't up to us to define because we may not live to see it manifest. In fact, we most assuredly won't live to see it. Part of eldering well is making peace with that fact.

Relationships are everything, which means community is everything. Relationship and community are who we are, they are who we become, and the lore shaped in reflection of them is what we give and how we are remembered.

INTROSPECTION

Exploring Your Lore

Take a few moments to sit with your experiences of lore by considering the following:

❋ How do you want to be remembered?

❋ What lore do you value?

❋ What stories of yourself in your current place-space best express you?

❋ What do your place-space beings, Allies, and Ancestors express about your lore?

❋ What lore have you carried that no longer serves you or your communities?

❋ What part of your lore needs to be rewritten to include empathy for beings you've not held in relationship?

❋ What new experiences could help expand your empathy?

✳ How does your lore situate into your cosmology?

✳ How do you recognize your Communal Heart?

✳ How does your lore demonstrate your wisdom?

✳

Addressing Shadow Lore

Take some time to address any shadow lore that comes up, both personal and collective. Peer into how you have allowed it to define you, and the places where you now differ from it. Consider how shadow lore provides the compost upon which to grow your new wisdom. Use the following prompts to reflect on shadow tending approaches from chapter 6, and craft ritual around sitting with the scars of that lore and what it has to teach going forward.

✳ How do you recognize shadow lore?

✳ Where do you feel it in your body?

✳ When sitting with specific lore, consider how it moves you along the fulfillment of your calling. Does it support your sacredness?

✳ Are you functioning as an elder when you uphold this lore? If not, where can you gain the skills to learn to do so?

✳ Where have you caused harm to yourself/others with this lore?

✳

Becoming a Fit Elder

In your thoughts of becoming a fit elder, explore the following:

✳ When you think of having caused harm, what feelings come up?

✳ Where do they situate in your body?

✳ Whose lore would best move you along your path to fit elderhood?

✳ How can you healthily, respectfully, and beneficially access that lore for all who dwell in your place-space?

✳ What does it mean for you to step aside to honor the lore of others? What would that look like?

Consider your feelings around having fit elders in your developmental years, defined as you feel led.

❋ What was your coming-of-age like? Express everything this question brings up, in detail.

❋ Did you have fit elders? If so, note who they were. If not, who did you look up to?

❋ In what ways did you elder yourself?

❋ Are there shadow parts still connected with those experiences? If so, what attention do they need?

❋ How did you become aware of your kinship with Nature?

❋ Do you consider yourself a fit elder now? Elaborate a bit.

❋ What resources support you to be a fit elder?

8
Standing in Harm's Danger
Engaging the Relationship between Agency and Impact

You say I turned out fine.
I think I'm still turning out.

AJR, "TURNING OUT"

When my twins were very little, they would get so upset to read stories where the balance of things was going along fine, until some character showed up and ruined everything. They just couldn't understand how someone could hurt someone else, steal, lie, or cause harm in some way. To explain it at their level, I said, "There's a Draco in every group." They got the reference to the bully in Harry Potter immediately but weren't at all happy with my response. It didn't soothe their discomfort with the story or sugar coat what could actually happen in their lives, but it became an anthem for them and was a conversation we had many times as they grew.

When they were older and experienced painful friend and group dynamics—the one left behind, the one outed or othered—I repeated myself but added, "And you're lucky if there's only one Draco in every group." By adolescence, when they started lying, were hurt by friends, and learned the consequences of violating others' boundaries, I added even further: "And maybe you're the Draco in the group."

Sooner or later in all of our lives, as human persons we have to face that pain is part of being in form. That's a difficult thing for many folx to accept because it flies in the face of our radical individualist capitalist myth and undermines the realities of what it really takes to survive in this culture. We don't want to deal with pain for any reason, even though we are surrounded by it all the time. When we have to face where we have caused pain, that dissonance is even more complex.

We have to come to terms with where we've used our agency to do harm, to ourselves and others, because in the end, it is always both. Anytime we harm someone, we harm ourselves, we harm the collective. And when we don't deal with the impact of that harm, we compile our legacy of ancestral trauma to be handed down. As animists we have to sit with our legacies of pain and the responsibility to our communities and the descendants not to carry them forward. In order not to carry them forward we must move among differently. We must break patterns by reconciling our ancestral trauma and by taking responsibility when we've caused harm.

LIVING IN THE SCAR

Moving among differently from our Ancestors, from our culture, and from how we've been moving often correlates to shadow work for many folx, which is why they are afraid of shadow tending: no one wants to admit they're the problem. Even when we can admit wrongdoing or that we have caused unintentional harm, we haven't been taught how to go forward in a stance of accountability. We haven't often had that modeled in settler culture. In fact, part of the supremacist perfectionist projection of this culture is not admitting wrongdoing, which, compounded over generations, creates warped justification (personal and systemic) around doing wrong. "This is just how my family has always done it." "Back then they didn't know any better." We've all heard the justifications.

As well, we more readily identify with being the one who has been harmed. Many of us have a history that includes betrayal, violence, pain, and trauma in our own lives, as well as felt ancestral components that we carry. Our cognitive dissonance from our own pain is such that without being able to express our own trauma, we often can't hold that we've harmed someone else or sit with how deeply the impact of that hurt goes, particularly if that harm is entrenched in systemic harm and bias.

In order to recognize harm that we cause intentionally or unintentionally, we have to again bring ourselves back from radical individualism and understand that our actions occur within relationship. Our actions ripple out impact, and in order to hold our agency with integrity, we must have empathy. Without it we can't have awareness of our relationship to harm, to those we have hurt. We must bring harm back into a collective context and take responsibility for all relationships involved—seen and unseen, real and imagined, intended and unintended, human and other-than-human person, and the deep legacy of impact. That particular step in our cultural maturity is imperative for humaning well.

We are the agents changing how we respond to having caused harm, and that change takes place in the scar. The scar is the point of impact, refashioned connective tissue that binds some version of who we were to who we are becoming in the same way it binds our shadow to our sacredness.

The scar is the place where we are no longer who we were. We are still in relationship with that version of ourselves, yet the relationship has changed and moved us into unfamiliar territory. It puts us in a place where we don't know who we are or how to move among, and the version of who we were before causing harm can't be accessed the same way anymore.

Yet, the nature of scar does not allow us to realize what lies beyond it. After it, our navigation for how to move forward isn't the same, and we aren't likely to have good intel on what it should be from our external systems—human family or settler culture. All we can discern about scar are the rough edges, limiting pain, and inability to recontextualize ourselves based on past patterns. In this way, scar becomes a portal into the potential of who we are and how we move among that didn't exist before harm happened. It brings the possibility of the moment, of ourselves being more than we could conceive of, previously. The Scar is the strongest lore supporting how we use our agency to wyrdweave our gift because it forces us to innovate our agency in ways we didn't know were possible until we had to.

Much like trauma, scar is not the challenging thing that happened; rather, it's what transpired in our lives after it happened. It's how the ecosystems of our body, mind, and soul seek to thrive and hold space for the pain of the event. And in many cases in broken-path settler culture, no space is held for pain, and this is why pain becomes trauma. In the way that pain originates trauma, wound begets scar. We cannot avoid the pain of scar, emotionally, physically, spiritually, though we can affect how we are in relationship with it.

Maybe among the more challenging aspects of eldering well and all it entails is that we find a way to be in the scar, not passively or temporarily, but in how we move among, ongoing. The same way that we cannot make scar "un-be," we must become fit elders *with scar*. To do so is the natural trajectory of soul in form as a human. The scar is part of who we become, and we can't omit it. It becomes part of our cosmology.

We have to learn to sit in the place that is uncomfortable and not fully fleshed out, that is messy, not easily or quickly solvable, and causes pain. Eldering well is to be in the middle of birth and death, innocence and maturity, soul and form, adversity and faith, gratitude and grief, wisdom and the unknowable. We have to evolve to a place where we can see that we are not just part of the scar but a custodian within it. The Gesturing Towards Decolonial Futures collective describes this between stance as not necessarily acquiring "knowledge that we didn't already have; rather, it may be a shift in our relationship to that knowledge.

This includes the courage and vulnerability to sit at the limits of knowledge and knowing, to risk being changed by what we come to know."[1] From this interstitial place we realize we all have the potential to be the problem, and we also all have the agency to do better.

But of course it's not that clear, is it? Those of us who have benefited most from the imbalance of our cultural systems have the hardest time realizing that benefit and thus have less impetus to generate change. We have less motivation to see what is problematic. We have not cultivated fortitude to tend scar, and we have more distraction from its wisdom. That includes those of us who have done so much work on the path of elderhood, even those of us reading these words. Those of us writing them.

OUR COLLUSION

American settler culture prides itself on not having an agreed upon cosmology. We cloak that projection in sayings like "life, liberty, and the pursuit of happiness" and "freedom of religion," while knowing some are more free than others (stretching all the way back to manifest destiny), honoring only Christian public observances and holidays, retrofitting how we move among to unnatural binaries, struggling against Puritanical work ethics and allegiance to myths of progress that determine our justness, and prioritizing projections of a heavenly afterlife over a sacred, Divine earthly ecosystem. We may not say that we have an agreed-upon cosmology, though anyone who functions in this society has adapted to the one at hand in order to survive. Just because it isn't a healthy cosmology doesn't mean it isn't a cosmology, and we have all paid into it in our own ways. We have all furthered it, even if unintentionally. We have all internalized it.

Where our collective cosmology fails us most is in interconnection with each other. Through it, we don't agree that we are Nature, that we are all in community all the time; thus we are absolved of living in a way that supports our interdependence and accountability to each other. Because we don't see ourselves in relationship, we haven't

prioritized emotional, physical, or spiritual technology that helps us succeed in community. In particular, we don't know how to recover from
having caused pain because if we move through life as a radical individual, we can believe that our actions have and deserve no ramifications.
We can continually believe scar will heal, and healing means reversion
to a previous experience of Self without conflict.

Much the way European-descended people left their indigeneity,
ancestral lands, spirits, and rituals behind, we also left our practical
technologies for sustaining community behind. This lack is very much
part of broken-path being. We haven't had healthy ancestral models
of community rupture and reparation handed down to us for how to
resolve harm and differences. We haven't created them the way that
other settler culture peoples have.

As a result, in this shared settler cosmology people don't feel part of
community, so we don't care about showing remorse when we've caused
harm, especially when it's someone or some community we don't value.
There's no impetus for changing how we behave or engage. Such disconnect means we may not even realize we caused harm or the scope of
it. Likewise, the folx most harmed are left without structural acknowledgment of that harm and are, by the inherent imbalance of the cosmology, left without resources to recover their power.

Problematic shared cosmology doesn't self-reorganize to prevent
harm. Without the folx most privileged by this cosmology initiating change and balance within it, nothing changes. The folx who are
harmed by it continue to be harmed by it. No space is held for the
wound, accountability, or reparation. When those don't exist in a cosmology, the harm perpetuates, and lack of awareness of community
shapes that cosmology to harm us all.

WHEN WE'RE THE DRACO

I wanted to title this chapter "Making Peace with Making Mistakes,"
though in reality I'm not really talking about mistakes—being wrong

or errant in some interaction—but the dynamic of harm that lives on after the exchange. I'm talking about how we respond when we've really screwed up. I'm not convinced that we make peace with making mistakes, and I'm even less convinced that we make peace with causing harm.

When we say we make peace with something, we typically mean that we end our discord with it, we resolve it. We reconcile the troubled dynamic that has held us together with dissonance. When our mistakes result in harm, that dynamic can have a lasting and incomprehensible impact, even well past apology and acknowledgment. The result of causing harm is a relationship, not necessarily one of our choosing, in which we have recontextualized our engagement of the dynamic and all involved. We may reconcile the dynamic of harm, though the harm itself and everyone impacted have their own agency. That dynamic has become scar, which persists on its own trajectory—quite possibly trajectories—for which we are still responsible.

Given that, we don't make peace with mistakes, we make scars with them. We create a space that didn't exist before, that is part of who we are going forward. We can't fully realize we're the Draco and the harmful impact of our agency until we've accepted the pain of the scar—our own and that which we caused.

In our time on this planet, it is not a question of if we cause harm. We do. We will, repeatedly. Our practices of embodiment and grounding and our rituals of tending must make room for that fact. With all our good intentions, we will screw up and handle that we screwed up poorly.

We will deny.

With all the shadow tending in the world, we will still grieve and grow, all the while ignoring aspects we don't like and don't want to deal with.

We will encounter biases we can't accept that we hold.

We will hurt other persons—human and other-than-human. We will hurt other persons, badly.

We will harm our ecosystems. We will devour them.

We will parent poorly.

We will teach harmful lore.

We will be called out.

We will be called in.

We will cancel and be canceled.

And we are the only ones who can still use our agency to respond differently. We are the only ones who can change how we are in relationship with harm and how we go forward with it.

THE PARALYSIS OF SHAME

When we talk about causing harm, we also confront shame. Shame is the state of being humiliated or disgraced when we act in a way that doesn't meet a social, cultural, or interpersonal expectation. We internalize it as losing respect or honor, and it can become a state of being that we carry with us for a long time. In fact, shame, by default, shapes our social engagement, ranging from dictating how we appear and engage, to who we value and engage. Shame—and our fear of it—can control our conduct, as it prompts our cooperation with the social consensus. It's an ancient scarlet letter that dictates how we behave in relationship, in community.

In settler culture, shame functions in different and sometimes conflicting ways. It can be an inhibitor of expressing sacredness, which keeps us subservient to norms. It can function as a motivator to gain approval based on how we adapt to those norms—even when we don't agree with them. Shame also functions as a trap in that when we feel it, it signals to us that we have violated a tenet of engagement. Our response is to freeze and withdraw, not unlike the gratitude-trauma connection we discussed in chapter 6.

From an ancestral perspective, generations-long unexpressed shame can function like survivor's guilt. We feel the reality of not having inflicted the pain, yet remain unable to thrive under the weight of it having happened.

Shame can be the very thing that stops us from attempting repair of harm we've caused. The impact of our culture of shame is always divisiveness, which reinforces radical individualism. It creates a bubble from which we don't feel we can be reintegrated, and often don't feel we deserve to be. In a dynamic in which we've caused harm, that isolation also prevents us from being accountable for our actions and leaves us cut off from resources that could teach us to do better.

STANDING IN DANGER

Some things can't be resolved, reconciled, or made peace with. They are scars, which by their obstinate nature, demand our attentiveness, our ongoing tending. For this reason when we have caused harm as animists, I suggest that instead of seeking to make peace with it that we learn to stand in the danger of those we have harmed.

In *The Dangerous Old Woman*, Clarissa Pinkola-Estés, Ph.D., says, "[Danger] in its oldest form . . . meant to protect. That literally you would say, 'You, stand in my danger. You stand in the aura surrounding me that is funded by my heart, my soul, and my spirit [and] that says certain things of this Earth are so precious they can never be allowed to be harmed or vanish from the face of this Earth.'"[2] To stand in each other's danger means by the strength of our relationship, of our interdependence, you are protected. WE are protected. It is recognition that we belong. When we stand in each other's danger, it means we see each other and put ourselves in the way of what would fundamentally disrupt our awareness of sacred order. It means when we are together, we are more protected.

It means that we live in such a way that our actions demonstrate the value of each other, that we know each other's agency, we prize each other's unique gift. In this stance, we honor that we are part of each other, and as such are responsible for each other's care. We acknowledge where our vitality and necessity for being on the planet are the same and vow to use our agency to protect that delicate interweaving.

As well, we commit to continue learning from danger, to use its wisdom as the cutting edge educator for us to ever seek ways of moving among that are aware, engaged, interconnected, and driven by interdependence.

To stand in the danger of someone we have harmed is yet another liminal expression of humaning, of honoring scars. We can't always make amends. We can't always save the state of a relationship. We can't return it to its former sheen, though we can stand in the danger of that relationship. We can open to learning greater depth of empathy, the humility of accountability, the nuance of consent, the rigor of duty, the comfort and sharp edges of trust, the fragility and strength of boundaries and needs, the work of repair, and the grounding of reflection. To stand in this healthy attachment is to bear our agency with greater awareness of the impact of agency itself. It is an extension of bearing our unique gift in that our gift is quite likely mostly for those we have harmed. Dwelling in the connective tissue of scar to tend reparation pushes our calling into territory we could not have conceived of prior to the harm caused yet we are led only to that ragged edge.

We call that betwixt stance many things—respect, reciprocity, trust. We call it the cycle of rupture, apology, and repair. We call it compassionate curiosity, research, and possibility.

To stand in the danger of those we have harmed means we will see the dynamic for exactly what it is and choose how to respond. How does standing in someone's danger look in practical terms? That could be highly personal and specific to the harm done. It may be undertaking a certain behavior or action to demonstrate changed engagement and reestablish trust. It may include public acknowledgment and demonstration of such. Whatever form it takes, it must be done within the context of the relationship and with consent, even if the relationship ends.

Every step of it will be allowing the emergence of Self as a fit elder. Good elders are still going to screw up. We're not always going to know what to do or how to respond. But we can keep moving among, rooted in our sacredness, in our human and nonhuman relationships, with our

Spirit Helpers, Allies, and Ancestors, pushing our agency forward as part of tending the scars we create.

Accepting these truths about ourselves, seeing who we are—personally and collectively—is a vital part of shifting our awareness of the broken path and what lies beyond it. We can't outcreate the break until we do. These acts of choosing how we respond to the harm we create is how other paths become possible.

Likewise, as a deep act of collective repair, we have to be able to hold the broken path and stand in its danger. We tend the hungry ghosts it's given us, the ways we've benefited from the break, the ways we perpetuate it. And we still have to have a vision of what is beyond the break, even if we don't know what that is, and live into it one generation at a time.

We don't know what possibilities lie beyond the broken path, though when we sit with what rising to eco-ensouled maturity means in settler culture, we know that eldering well is the only way we get there. And that means not just reinventing our understanding of elder but also of the kind of world we want to leave behind, the legacy we are creating. Our task is to stand in the danger of possibility, in the trickiness of scar, and do just that.

INTROSPECTION

Considering Trust, Accountability, Forgiveness, and Reciprocity

When you sit with all the dynamics this reading has stirred, consider who you trust to be honest with you. Consider your ability to be honest with yourself. Consider your willingness to change, and who on your Dream Team can assist with education around that.

❋ Who do you go to for accountability?
❋ Who do you trust to tell you the truth about yourself? Your work? Your past?

❀ How do you allow the process of apology and repair?

❀ What does forgiving someone who has harmed you look like?

❀ What does forgiving yourself look like?

❀ What is your relationship with being forgiven? With forgiving?

❀ What three boundaries are most important to you? Sit with each individually to determine if they need updating or releasing.

❀ How do you assess your needs? Which of them need to be filled by others? Which ones need to be filled by you? How do you carry that data into your relationships?

❀ How do you engage reciprocity in relationships? Who determines that exchange is balanced?

❀ With what relationships have you not engaged in reciprocity?

❀ How does reciprocity affect how you feel about someone? About the relationship?

❈

Considering Your Relationship to Shame

Shame interferes with our awareness of sacred order, our agency, and the bearing of our calling, all of which support the break and everything it entails. We have to do the emotional, interpersonal, and soul work at its root, so that we can show up better in community.

Consider your relationship to shame and what events have left you feeling ashamed in your life.

❀ How do you experience shame?

❀ Where does it show up in your body?

❀ How does shame influence how you talk to yourself? To your ecosystem?

❀ What relationships have been most affected by shame in your life? Pay particular attention to the relationship between a scar and shame.

❀ Where are you unable to live into the possibility of scar because you feel you don't deserve to?

✳ Where has your lore been coded with shame?

✳ How do your limitations with shame contribute to the broken path?

✳ How do they hold you back from deeper relationship? From your calling?

✦

Humaning leaves a mark. Humans leave a mark. It is what we do, to everything we engage. Not because we intend to but because form is a realm of agency. Agency is impact, and impact leaves a scar. What is impacted reorganizes and becomes something other. Earth was made by elements bumping into each other. It is sustained and furthered by elements—by us—bumping into each other. Life stretches from those points of impact toward the possibility that scar promises.

Having the most accessible, applicable agency in this realm also means we have the greatest potential to cause harm. The best we can do is be mindful of how we apply our agency to tend its impact, to tend the scars that we leave.

Even a scar as big as a whole path.

Suggested Resources

These resources include works from some of my most influential teachers on animism, energy tending, spiritual ecology, decolonization, racial justice, and the indigenous roots of Europe.

BOOKS AND ESSAYS

Ancestral Journeys: The Peopling of Europe from the First Venturers to the Vikings by Jean Manco

Animism: Respecting the Living World by Graham Harvey

The Art of Community: Seven Principles for Belonging by Charles Vogl

Boundaries & Protection by Pixie Lighthorse

Braiding Sweetgrass: Indigenous Wisdom, Scientific Knowledge, and the Teachings of Plants by Robin Wall Kimmerer

Come of Age: The Case for Elderhood in a Time of Trouble by Stephen Jenkinson

The Dawn of Everything: A New History of Humanity by David Graeber and David Wengrow

Decolonizing Trauma Work: Indigenous Stories and Strategies by Renee Linklater

Deep Liberation: Shamanic Teachings for Reclaiming Wholeness in a Culture of Trauma by Langston Kahn

Entangled Life: How Fungi Make Our Worlds, Change Our Minds, and Shape Our Futures by Merlin Sheldrake

The Handbook of Contemporary Animism by Graham Harvey

The Healing Wisdom of Africa: Finding Life Purpose Through Nature, Ritual, and Community by Maladoma Patrice Somé

The Hidden Life of Trees: What They Feel, How They Communicate; Discoveries from a Secret World by Peter Wohlleben

Joyous Resilience: A Path to Individual Healing and Collective Thriving in an Inequitable World by Anjuli Sherin

Me and White Supremacy: Combat Racism, Change the World, and Become a Good Ancestor by Layla F. Saad

My Grandmother's Hand: Racialized Trauma and the Pathway to Mending Our Hearts and Bodies by Resmaa Menakem.

Prayers of Honoring Grief by Pixie Lighthorse

Sacred Ceremony: How to Create Ceremonies for Healing, Transitions, and Celebrations by Steven D. Farmer

Sand Talk: How Indigenous Thinking Can Save the World by Tyson Yunkaporta

So You Want to Talk about Race by Ijeoma Oluo

These Wilds Beyond Our Fences: Letters to My Daughter on Humanity's Search for Home by Bayo Akomolafe

The Well of Remembrance: Rediscovering the Earth Wisdom Myths of Northern Europe by Ralph Metzner

"White Privilege: Unpacking the Invisible Knapsack" by Peggy McIntosh

ORGANIZATIONS, PODCASTS, AND ONLINE COURSEWORK

Cultural Somatics Institute (website)

DarkSky International (website)

Decolonial Healing, Dr. Rosales Meza (website)

Facing Human Wrongs: Navigating Paradoxes and Complexities of Social and Global Change (blog)

Fair Folk, Danica Boyce (podcast)

For the Wild (podcast)

Gesturing Towards Decolonial Futures (website)

Good Ancestor, Layla F. Saad (podcast)

Nordic Animism, Rune Hjarnø Rasmussen (podcast)

Othering and Belonging Institute at UC Berkley (website)

Science & Nonduality (website)

The Last Mask Center for Shamanic Healing (website)

The Sacred Flame, Mathias Nordvig (podcast)

What Happened to the Tribes of Europe, John Trudell (YouTube)

White Awake (website)

Notes

INTRODUCTION. THE PROBLEM OF ANIMISM

1. Graham Harvey, *Animism: Respecting the Living World*, 2nd ed. (London: Hurst & Company, 2017), xvii.
2. Joseph Vadella, "Origins of 'Human,'" *Joseph's Passion Blog*, September 8, 2017.
3. Rune Hjarnø Rasmussen, "What Is Animism," YouTube, 5:25.
4. Graham Harvey, *Animism*, 1.
5. Lyla June, "My people pay attention to the movement of the stars, the sun, the moon and the shadows to be in relationship with time," lylajune Instagram, December 1, 2020.

I. OUR CULTURAL RELATIONSHIP TO ANIMISTIC ELDERHOOD

1. Evelyn Rysdyk, *The Norse Shaman* (Rochester Vt.: Destiny Books, 2016), 30.
2. Laura Udesky, "The Wisdom of Trauma: Gabor Maté, Peter Levine in Conversation about How the Body Heals from Trauma," PACEsConnection, June 23, 2021.
3. Bettany Hughes, "How Christians Destroyed the Ancient World," *New York Times*, June 18, 2018.
4. Mathias Nordvig, *The Sacred Flame* podcast, episode "Ancestors: Spirits of the Land," February 26, 2023; 28:02.
5. Women's Earth Alliance and Native Youth Sexual Health Network, *Violence on the Land, Violence on Our Bodies: Building an Indigenous Response to Environmental Violence*, Women's Earth Alliance, June 18, 2016.

6. Runic John, *The Book of Seidr: The Native English and Northern European Shamanic Tradition* (Somerset, UK: Capall Bann Publishing, 2004), 40–42.

7. "What Is the Doctrine of Discovery?" Doctrine of Discovery (website) last modified September 26, 2022.

8. Steven D. Farmer, *Sacred Ceremony: How to Create Ceremonies for Healing, Transitions, and Celebrations* (Vista, Calif.: Hay House, 2002), 6.

2. REPAIRING THE HUMAN-NATURE RELATIONSHIP

1. Tala Khanmalek, "A Revolution Capable of Healing Our Wounds: An Interview with Aurora Levins Morales," *nineteen sixty nine: an ethnic studies journal* 2, no. 1 (2013).

2. Ashish Kothari, et al., eds. *Pluriverse: A Post-Development Dictionary* (New Delhi: Tulika Books, in association with AuthorsUpFront, 2019).

3. Tyson Yunkaporta, *Sand Talk: How Indigenous Thinking Can Save the World*. (New York: Harper One, 2020), 51.

4. Maria Kvilhaug, *Fylgjur: Guardian Spirits and Ancestral Mothers*, Blade Honor, January 29, 2020.

5. Runic John, *The Native English and Northern European Shamanic Tradition* (Somerset, UK: Capall Bann Publishing, 2004), 187.

6. The Old Norse World, s.v. "vǫrðr."

7. The Berkana half-month rune, based on runic calendar calculations done by Nigel Pennick in *Runic Astrology: Starcraft and Timekeeping in the Northern Tradition* (Northhamptonshire: Thorsons, 1990).

8. Vanessa Taylor, *Exploring the Ethnosphere*, Berkeley Public Policy, MPD, 2015.

3. ALLOWING THE EMERGENCE OF SACRED SELF

1. "Twice As Long—Life Expectancy around the World," Our World in Data, last modified in October 2019.

2. Dictionary.com, s.v. "sacren."

3. *Britannica*, s.v. "sacred."

4. Kendra Cherry, "Ego as the Rational Part of Personality," Verywell Mind (website), May 09, 2020.

5. *Merriam-Webster*, s. v. "skera."

4. PRIORITIZING EMBODIMENT AND GROUNDING

1. Kimberly Ann Johnson, "Spirit Work, Conspiracies, Elderhood and Grief with Stephen Jenkinson, Part One," episode 135, SoundCloud, September, 2021.
2. Langston Kahn, *Deep Liberation: Shamanic Teachings for Reclaiming Wholeness in a Culture of Trauma* (Berkeley: North Atlantic Books, 2021), 41.

5. ENGAGING RITUALS FOR CARING
AND ACCOUNTABILITY

1. "I Consent to the Law of Mother Earth" with Woman Stand Shining (Pat McCabe), YouTube, May 14, 2019.

6. HONORING OUR CALLING TO
TEND COMMUNITY

1. Robin Wall Kimmerer, *Braiding Sweetgrass: Indigenous Wisdom, Scientific Knowledge, and the Teachings of Plants* (Minneapolis, Minn.: Milkweed Editions, 2013), 115.
2. Odelya Gertel Kraybill, "The Neuroscience of Gratitude and Trauma," *Psychology Today*, January 31, 2020.
3. Kraybill, "Neuroscience of Gratitude."
4. Kraybill, "Neuroscience of Gratitude."
5. Charles Vogl, *The Art of Community: Seven Principles for Belonging* (Oakland, Calif.: Beret-Koehler Publishers, 2016), 9, 12.
6. Vogl, *The Art of Community*.

7. PASSING ON OUR LORE WITH COMPASSION

1. Bayo Akomolafe, transcribed from the course The Wandering, Winding Way of the Wound, module 3, Yoruba Indigenous and Other Productions of Wellbeing, 2022.
2. Tyson Yunkaporta, *Sand Talk: How Indigenous Thinking Can Save the World* (New York: HarperOne, 2020), 148.
3. *Merriam-Webster*, s.v. "empathy."

8. STANDING IN HARM'S DANGER

1. Vanessa Andreotti, Rene Susa, and Dougald Hine, "Depth Conversations," *Gesturing Towards Decolonial Futures* (website), February 21, 2021.
2. Clarissa Pinkola-Estes, *The Dangerous Old Woman: Myths and Stories of the Wise Woman Archetype* (Louisville, Colo.: Sounds True, 2010), unabridged audiobook, 18:04.

Index